Boat Living

Boat Living

by Jack Wiley

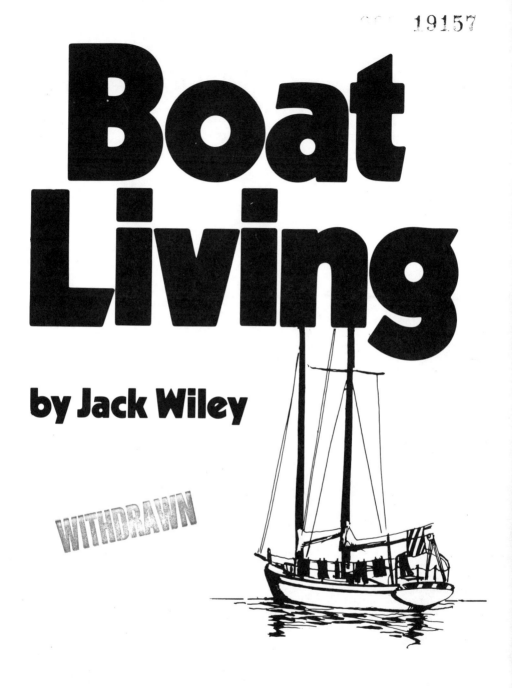

International Marine Publishing Company
Camden, Maine

CONTENTS

Boat
Living

INTRODUCTION

There has long been a romantic notion associated with living aboard boats, but until rather recently only a few people in the United States managed to make the dream a reality. Today the situation is vastly different. Thousands of individuals, couples, and families are now living aboard boats, and others are taking up this alternative way of life. The basic idea is that a boat is substituted for housing ashore.

Why are people making the switch? Here are some of the reasons:

(1) It's a means of escaping the high cost of a "conventional" home on land — whether it be a house, apartment, condominium, or mobile home. The common belief that living aboard a boat is *only* for the idle rich just isn't true. Many people have actually reduced the cost of living by moving from a land home to a boat.

(2) It's a means of escaping "the rat race." For many, the sea offers the last hope for freedom. Air pollution, overpopulation, jammed freeways (the list could go on for pages) are driving an ever-increasing number of people back to the sea.

(3) Many have found that boat living, especially in a modern marina, is like nothing else available. Some people have described it as being the equivalent of a perpetual vacation paradise.

(4) Modern boats, which feature many of the comforts and conveniences typical of land housing, have attracted many to a life afloat.

All ages have taken to this alternative way of life, including families with young children and retired people. The only age requirement seems to be that the person be young at heart. Actual age is unimportant.

Lifestyles of people living in boats vary widely. Some are "boat bums" who live on practically nothing; others spend a great deal of money and live in luxury. Most are somewhere between these extremes.

For some, the boat serves only as a floating home tied to a dock and rarely, if ever, is used for any other purpose. Others use their boat for recreational purposes as well, spending at least some time away from the dock. Some have made cruising to faraway places, and even around the world, a way of life.

Yet, for every person who has lived in a boat, there must be thousands dreaming about just such a life. What makes the bridge between dream and reality especially difficult to cross is the lack of specific information on what life on a boat is really like and how to make the switch from land to water. I know, because I was once in the middle of Illinois, dreaming about another way, an alternative, and an intensive search of the published boating materials revealed almost nothing about living in a boat. Now and then I found a relevant article, but it usually tended to leave more questions unanswered than it answered. In the end, I still had only a vague idea of what boat life would be like, what type and size of boat would be best for me, what difficulties and problems might be involved, or how much it would cost. And the little information I did find was in widely scattered sources.

As I sit writing this, I feel the gentle rock of the *Sea Puppy* (she's a 21½-foot Westerly Warwick sloop, built in England). The sun is shining, the window view is unbeatable. A motel near the marina has a similar view, except that the rooms there are fifty dollars a day and up. I manage on a tiny fraction of that.

How did I bridge the gap? One thing is certain: I didn't do it by the most direct route. Had I only known in the dream stage what I have since learned, I could have saved much time and money and made many fewer wrong turns on the way from dream to reality.

Now I am attempting to write the book for which I searched in vain. It has if-I-had-it-to-do-over-again hindsight. However, the information included comes from many sources in addition to my own experience of over three and a half years living aboard the *Sea Puppy*. Many tips and ideas come from the hundreds of other live-aboarders I have met along the way. I have long had an interest in boats, and I suppose much of the material is the result of my passion for hanging around boatyards and waterfront areas. Useful too, I believe, were my boatbuilding endeavors. While still in high school I built an 11½-foot pram, and about six years ago I constructed a 30-foot Piver-designed trimaran.

This book is a guide for anyone who is uncertain about how to go about becoming a boat dweller. While it is intended primarily for those who want to make a boat their residence in lieu of a land house, much of the material should also be helpful to those who desire to try it on a more limited scale, perhaps during weekends and vacation periods. This is a how-to book for selecting, acquiring, and living aboard all types of boats.

1 FROM DREAM TO REALITY

The question might be raised, "Isn't living aboard a boat a return to a more primitive life?" In some cases it is, although with a modern, well-equipped boat it need not be. Some boats are permanently moored, and the living in them is what might be called "settled." Other boats move around, their owners leading a wandering life. The lifestyles of some boat dwellers could be considered primitive, at least in the sense that theirs is a life closer to nature; but some people manage to take along many of the so-called conveniences of modern living. An apt comparison can be made with a life on wheels. There are those who are living in old, rundown bread vans under something akin to camping conditions; others have large, modern motor homes with all the amenities of an efficiency apartment.

Brief history

The name of the first boat dweller remains a matter of conjecture. Certainly he lived long ago. Quite likely he was using a boat for fishing or transportation and decided it would be more convenient to live where he worked.

In many parts of the world today, there are large groups of people living in boats. A large part of Hong Kong's population, for example, traditionally lives in junks and houseboats, probably because of overcrowded conditions on land, among other factors.

The Bajau Laut, a large group of people in the Philippines, make extensive use of houseboats and houses built over the sea on stilts. The waters are shallow, and these types of housing are quite practical. The local people often use stilts to negotiate the shallow waters between the shore and their dwellings.

The Aymara Indians of Lake Titicaca, in Peru, live in houses made from and floating on platforms of totora reeds. They make their boats by lashing together tapered bundles of these reeds.

In Manaus, Brazil, is another example of a floating community. Houses, walkways, and even restaurants are built on logs floating out from the edge of the Río Negro.

Closer to the United States are the *vagabundos del mar* (vagabonds of the sea) in the Sea of Cortez (Gulf of California). It all started, according to one source, when some Yaqui Indians deserted the land for a more pleasant life on the sea in their sailing canoes. That was more than a century ago. In more recent times, they have been imitated by a number of Mexicans who did not like, among other things, working for others and being subjected to landside rules and laws. Among them are people from all walks of life, including peons, college professors, and medical doctors. A few U. S. citizens have also joined them. In essence, they have broken their ties with land to follow a life of greater freedom on the sea. Their possessions are few; their contact with the land is generally limited to occasional trading. Most of their needs are provided by the sea.

In the United States there have long been boat dwellers tucked away here and there. In Mark Twain's day, there were people living on rafts equipped with crude shacks for protection from the weather. This existence has been romanticized in literature, poetry, and song. The first boat dwellers in the United States probably were people who used boats to make a living, but others eventually took to it purely as a viable alternative to having a house on land. On inland waters, shanty boats became more and more popular not only for vacation places but also for permanent living accommodations. By the 1930s, living in boats was the subject of a number of magazine and newspaper articles. It shared the same air of romance often associated with the land vagabond.

But it seems to have taken the mass production of boats with more comforts and conveniences to bring boat living up to a standard acceptable to a large group of people. In the 1950s the boating boom was on, and as the popularity of boating grew, increasing numbers of people took to living aboard boats.

It is interesting to note that the current popularity of living aboard boats is not limited to the United States. For example, there are over 200 boats and floating homes along the Seine in Paris inhabited by individuals, couples, and families, and over 3,000 in the waterways of Amsterdam.

Perhaps the single most important development leading to this boating boom was fiberglass, which made at least semi-mass-production possible. Here was a material that also eliminated many of the problems inherent in other boatbuilding materials, allowing the construction of boats that required only a minimum of maintenance. This is not to say that fiberglass is a perfect boatbuilding material, or that it might not be replaced someday by a far superior material. It probably will be. But today fiberglass is *the* material for boatbuilding. This is true in spite of the fact that some publications make it sound as though ferrocement and its variations have taken over. A look at the boats currently in use, and the new and used boats available to the potential buyer, quickly shows that this is not the case.

Statistics

There are almost no statistics about live-aboard boats and their inhabitants. The more common sources fail even to recognize the existence of live-aboarders; if they do, they list them under "Other." Boating organizations that claim to have comprehensive boating statistics would not even venture a guess as to the number of people currently living in boats in the United States.

Most questionnaires about housing make no mention of boats. People whose boats are more or less permanently moored in one location are likely to go uncounted. If a live-aboarder moves around without maintaining a home port, it is even less likely that his or her existence will be included in population statistics. In fact, living aboard a boat and moving from port to port is an excellent way to "get lost," if that is what is desired. One man I know was facing a divorce suit, and he didn't want anyone to know his whereabouts. He managed this easily for eight months by cruising up and down the West Coast of the United States.

From my own experience, however, along the Florida, Alabama, Mississippi, and Louisiana coasts of the Gulf of Mexico and along the West Coast of the United States, especially California, I know there are many more people living in boats than might be commonly believed, but I could not guess how many there might be. At some marinas where I thought at first there were none, I discovered after a while that there were dozens. A growing number of "sneak-aboarders" are living aboard boats without telling marina operators. For example, at the Marina del Rey in Los Angeles, about 390 of the 5,800 slips are occupied by boats with one or more official residents, but one of these individuals told me he believes that there are at least an equal number of "unofficial" residents. There seem to be two main reasons for secrecy: to get around bans and quotas and to avoid paying special fees that are charged by many marinas.

Locations

Where do boat dwellers live in the United States? In general, wherever the law and the weather permit, on both inland and ocean waters. Most of the latter are well-protected waters. As might be expected, the greatest number live in warmer climates. But there are also some people who endure winters of snow, ice, and freezing temperatures. There are also the migrants who go north in the summer and south in the winter. A growing number of people cruise around the world.

Places where natural harbors and protected anchorages are plentiful tend to attract the greatest concentrations of live-aboarders, and these places usually have the fewest rules. Restrictive laws generally are passed as soon as the demand for marina slips and moorings in an area exceeds the supply. Florida seems to be the state with the best conditions for living aboard boats, and it probably is the state with the most people doing it.

Types of boats

What types of boats do people live in? Essentially, anything that floats and has living accommodations. This ranges from permanently moored floating houses, which are presently booming in popularity, to power and sail (and combination) boats with considerable boating potential. It would be my guess that most people live in houseboats. But there are many places where conditions make houseboats unsafe, so more seaworthy craft are required.

Is boat living for you?

Before you face the practical realities of acquiring a boat, moving aboard, living aboard, and supporting yourself, you must decide if this is really what you want. For the thousands who dream of living

Figure 1. *Built sturdily and moored permanently, this floating house has no means of self-propulsion. (Photo by author.)*

aboard a boat, this is the step that probably stops most from achieving the reality. Many who now live in boats feel that the most difficult step was making a firm decision, a commitment, to do it.

How do you make the decision before selling out on land living? I know of no 100-percent-certain method, but there are a number of things you can do to help make sure the decision will be the right one. I'm not trying to push this lifestyle for everyone. It's not for everyone. Even if we disregard all of the people who are not even dreaming of such a life, there are still many who, in reality, would not be suited to the life. As I see it, people frequently make one of two wrong decisions: (1) someone who is ideally suited to living aboard decides not to do it, and (2) someone who is unsuited decides to do it.

To make an intelligent decision, you must have as much information as possible. In many cases it's possible to try out the life (for example, by renting a boat and living in her for a period of time) be-

Figure 2. *The Gulfstar 41-foot offshore sailing auxiliary. Her flexible living arrangements make her an ideal live-aboard boat. (Courtesy Gulfstar, Inc.)*

fore making a definite decision to buy a boat. Those who plunge into the life, only to find that it isn't for them, usually flee back to land after a costly trial.

On the other hand, thousands have found boat living to be idyllic, even better than they had imagined. And that is something in this era of high-pressure advertising when things have a habit of not being what we were led to believe they would be.

Requirements for success

While there are some exceptions, I have found that people who make a success of living in a boat generally possess the following characteristics:

(1) Love for the water. They like to look at it, swim in it, boat on it — and not just in their dreams. Take a careful look at this requirement for success. Apply it to yourself. Whenever you have a chance, do you head for the water? Do you truly enjoy, or merely tolerate, activities connected with the water? This love-for-water requirement may seem too obvious to mention, but some of the greatest live-aboard disasters have been caused by hatred of, rather than love for, the water.

(2) Love of an active life. Boat living generally offers an active existence, especially if real boating is also involved. Most boat dwellers, for example, are involved in such active endeavors as cruising, fishing, skin and scuba diving, and bicycling, not to mention the upkeep of the boat. If a person would rather lead a passive existence, then a rocking chair may be a better bet than a boat. But this does not mean you have to be young — only active. Many senior citizens have adopted the lifestyle with complete success.

(3) Ability to live happily with a minimum of possessions. Even in a relatively large boat, there is room for only a small fraction of the possessions normally housed in the typical land dwelling. Many people consider this to be one of the advantages of living in a boat. Possessions are exactly what they want to evade. But others who try a life afloat find it impossible to live without more possessions than the boat could possibly hold, and they flee back to land.

(4) Desire to escape the rat race. This requirement doesn't always apply, since it is sometimes possible to stay in the rat race. But most boat dwellers want to escape, at least to some extent, the rat race so commonly associated with land living. If a person wants to "keep up

with the Joneses," living aboard a boat is probably not advisable, although there is a certain status attached to owning some of the more luxurious floating homes. Of course many socialites have yachts, but these are seldom their full-time residences. One would think that everyone would want to escape the rat race, but apparently many people thrive on it and would miss the smog, the congested traffic, the commuting, and the cutthroat jobs if they were away from it all.

(5) Ability to live in confined space. Even a fairly large boat, say 40 feet, will probably not have the interior space of the average small apartment. While many comforts and conveniences can be fitted into boats, it is necessary to squeeze them into a small space. If more than one person is living aboard the boat, additional complications often arise.

Other requirements associated with successful boat living include an ability to live without "roots" on land, a desire to be independent (at least more independent than is typical of land living), and a willingness to give up some things that are impossible or impractical in a boat, such as a private yard for children, or a large workshop, or a garden (although gardening on a small scale is possible on permanently moored floating houses and houseboats). And, unless you have a very large boat, the grand piano will have to stay behind. Successful boat living, then, involves giving up some things in order to gain others. It's also important that all members of the family or group concerned possess the same qualifications for success.

Reasons for failures

To take up life in a boat and then find it is not for you is a costly mistake.

Below are some of the reasons given by people who tried living aboard a boat and returned to living on land:
(1) Too uncomfortable
(2) Not enough space (Couples found that in confined quarters they detested each other.)
(3) Too restrictive an existence
(4) Too isolated
(5) Lack of roots
(6) Nostalgia for previous lifestyle

   (7) Unsuitable environment for raising children

   (8) Job transfer

   (9) More costly endeavor than anticipated

  (10) Too much trouble with boat

  (11) Gradual dissatisfaction with the water

   I suspect that seasickness (nausea and malaise provoked by the motion of a vessel at sea) has also been responsible for some failures. Some people suffer from seasickness even while living in a boat moored in calm, well-protected waters.

Sampling the life

   This book should give considerable insight into what the life will be like, but if you have never tried living in a boat, I suggest that you rent a houseboat for two weeks or more. While this may be far too short a period to decide if living aboard is definitely for you, it's generally long enough to dissuade those who are totally unsuited to the life. Even though a person may have some other type of boat in mind, I suggest a houseboat, because that is one of the few types of craft that can be rented by inexperienced skippers. Also, the rental rates tend to be lower than for power cruisers and auxiliary sailboats with living accommodations. Rental houseboats are available in a number of areas of the United States. *Family Houseboating's Houseboat Rental Guide* (published by *Family Houseboating*, 10148 Riverside Drive, North Hollywood, California 91602) covers houseboat rentals in all parts of the country. During vacation seasons, there is a heavy demand for houseboats, so make reservations as early as possible.

   Try to rent a houseboat that has approximately the same accommodations and interior size as the boat you intend to purchase if the trial proves satisfactory. Keep in mind that a 35-foot houseboat, for instance, probably has a much larger interior than a 35-foot power cruiser or sailboat. (Relative size is discussed more fully in Chapter 3.)

   If you are eager to get back to land living long before the rental period is over, then boat living is probably not for you, and you've discovered this without spending a great deal of money — no more than the cost of the vacation. If, on the other hand, you enjoy the experiment, then you may be a good candidate for living full-time in a boat. Again, it should be stressed that the conclusion should be agreed upon by all who will take part in the venture. It is a mistake for you to pretend that you like it when you don't, even to please a mate. If you don't like it after a few weeks, what will it be like after a year or two? Though it may be possible to "learn to like it," I doubt if many do. I think that most often it is immediately apparent whether a person is suited to the lifestyle or not. Consider also that if the houseboat was rented during a period of favorable weather, she may be even less tolerable during cold and rainy months.

A trial period in a houseboat should give ample opportunity for meeting and talking to some year-round residents. Even if it is impractical to rent or charter a boat, try to talk and visit with some people in the area where you intend to live. A great deal can be learned from them about what to expect. This is a good way to find out if there are any special problems involved and also what types of boats are most suitable for the area.

Who are the live-aboarders?

It is helpful to anyone contemplating life in a boat to take a look at the backgrounds of the live-aboarders. The categories below are based on my own observations, and I have no way of knowing how many people fall into each group.

(1) Some began their lives in boats. Their parents were live-aboarders and they continued in the life, like a circus act being passed down in a family from generation to generation. But this accounts for only a small percentage of those whom I have known or heard about or read about. Even one generation back, there were relatively few families in boats, compared with today.

(2) Some were part of recreational-boating families. They grew up with boating in their leisure time, saw the life going on around them, and later decided it was what they wanted.

(3) Some trace their initial interest to a period at sea in the Navy or Coast Guard, or to time spent as commercial fishermen, or to involvement with some other boating occupation, or even to a trip across an ocean in a passenger ship. While some who retire from boating occupations wish to continue to live afloat, others move as far away from the water as possible.

(4) Many come to the life after taking up boating on a recreational basis. This gradually led them to become full-time live-aboarders.

For many, living aboard is a way of being closer to what they once enjoyed.

(5) Some of the most dedicated people I have encountered were dreaming of boat life before they had had any actual taste of boating, much less any experience living in a boat. While some of the greatest successes have come about in this way, so too have some of the most profound failures.

Most of the people do seem to fall into various social categories as well. There are those called boat bums or vagabonds, who have found boat living to be better than the land equivalent. They generally own little more than an old boat, spend little money, and work as little as possible. It sounds quite romantic, but many people, especially hard workers, are quite prejudiced against this group. My own experience with them is that they tend to be friendly and much more honest than they are given credit for. Among them are professional people who were once quite successful, in terms of making a lot of money. Others never had much money. They seem to ask little more than tolerance, and tend to make use of free anchorages whenever possible. All in all, I believe that they find a better life at sea than on land.

As we move up the economic ladder, we find people who have more expensive (though not always better) boats. They also work harder and longer at making money. They generally live at the less expensive marinas and moorings. Perhaps the largest group are people who have steady jobs or incomes, for instance, from retirement funds. There are also professional people who tend to have larger and more expensive craft, and they generally live at the better marinas and yacht clubs. Mixed in with all categories, however, are those who somehow have money without working.

The one outstanding feature I've noticed is that live-aboarders tend to be individualists, although even here there are some exceptions.

Single men living alone seem to make up the largest group of boat dwellers. They are followed closely by couples (married or otherwise). Families with children probably follow, but in the area I'm most familiar with (southern California), it is difficult to find a marina where children are allowed. I know of one family who tried living in San Diego Bay. They had to live at anchor, because no marina would admit them. Finally, they trailed the boat to Florida. The last I heard, they had no difficulty finding a marina that would accept them, which I was glad to hear, since every member of that family was friendly and considerate, even when discriminated against by marina operators. Within my experience, there are few single women living alone in boats. There are also singles of the same sex, both men and women, who share boat living expenses, although again the numbers seem to be few.

After the decision

If, after due consideration, you decide that a boat is just what you've been seeking as a home, then you can proceed to make it a reality. And that brings us to the matter of money, which is the subject of the next chapter.

2 MONEY MATTERS

Boat living has two primary prerequisites: (1) acquisition of a boat and (2) the means to support life aboard her. This chapter gives a general idea of costs involved. More specific information on costs and ways of reducing them is included in later chapters. Since lifestyles vary so greatly, the information is intended only as a guideline, and it must be modified to fit each situation.

Acquiring a boat

One way to acquire a boat is to pay for her in full at the time of purchase; another is to obtain a loan (usually a down payment is required) and pay off the mortgage while living aboard; and a third way is to reduce the cost of the boat by building all or part of her yourself.

People use ingenious methods for obtaining boats, leading me to believe that there is at least some truth in the saying, "If you want something badly enough, you can have it."

Ways of acquiring a boat without going into debt should be considered first. Below are some of the possibilities:

(1) Trading a house or other property, directly or indirectly, for a boat. A number of people have used this approach when they retired. Many people by this time own a house that, in many cases, will more than cover the cost of a boat. Usually it is advantageous to sell the house or other property and then purchase the boat with cash rather than make a direct trade, but there are times when a satisfactory trade can be arranged.

(2) Saving one's money, by careful planning and economizing, until the boat can be purchased. I believe that this method is more practical than it may sound at first. I've known several working

couples who managed to save enough for a boat within as little as two years, and they thus avoided making payments over long periods of time, which might have resulted in paying twice the price of the boat.

(3) Building a boat, either all or in part. The possibilities are detailed in Chapter 7. The main principle involved is that the boat should be built as the money becomes available. It's like buying on time without paying any interest. In most cases, the total cost will be less than that of a factory equivalent. There is also the possibility of launching and living aboard a boat when she is only partially completed: I know of some do-it-yourself boatyards where people live in their boats while building them.

Many people borrow to finance their boats. In most cases, a steady income will be needed and payments are made on the boat instead of on a house or condominium (or instead of rent payments). Even with today's inflation, it's possible to find many boats suitable for homes (providing your tastes don't run too high) for under $15,000.

As a hypothetical situation, let's assume that a suitable boat is available for $15,000. While it may be possible to get by with a down payment of 10 percent of the cost of a new boat or 20 percent for a used one, we'll assume that the buyer has enough cash to pay one-third down — or, in this case, $5,000. He will need to borrow $10,000. As a member of a credit union, he can get either a seven-year or a 10-year loan at 10 percent annual simple interest. (The true annual percentage rate (A.P.R.) will be much higher, since the annual simple interest is paid for the full amount of the original loan for the entire loan period and, as payments are made, the borrower will only have use of part of the money.) Over a period of seven years, the monthly payments would be $202.39; over a 10-year period, $166.67. Notice that in either case the interest averages out to $1,000 a year for the period of the loan. In the first case, the total interest is $7,000; in the second, $10,000. To this is often added a credit life insurance policy, which increases each monthly payment by a few dollars.

In many states a sales tax must be paid on the cost of the boat at the time of purchase. If the tax rate were six percent, for example, $900 would have to be paid, along with the $5,000 down, on the $15,000 boat. There will be other expenses, such as registration, but since these have to be paid for as long as the boat is owned, they will be considered later in this chapter under "Living expenses."

In the purchase of houses and condominiums, twenty- and thirty-year loans are common. However, boat loans seldom run more than 10 or 12 years. Refinancing (borrowing money to pay off the balance of the original loan) may be possible, but of course it will increase the total amount of interest paid.

Some people rent boats rather than buy them. I've also known of people who obtained living privileges in exchange for maintaining the boat or doing some other work. In most cases, however, boat dwellers purchase their own boats.

Prices of almost all categories of boats (new, used, home-built) have increased alarmingly in the last few years. For this and many other reasons, it is almost impossible to give completely accurate information about how much one might cost. While I have known people who have purchased boats adequate for their purposes for as little as $500, most people would consider these boats unsuitable. On the present market, most people will have to think in terms of $500 or more for each foot of boat length overall. I'm not sure what the highest price that anyone has ever paid for a boat home is, but I'm quite sure it's more money than I could expect to earn in several lifetimes. This book assumes you will have to take money into careful consideration, though not necessarily to the extreme of settling on a $500 boat.

Living expenses

Beyond the boat-loan payments, if any, the main recurring expenses include marina or anchorage fees, property and/or use taxes (if applicable in the area where the boat is located), insurance, boat maintenance, utilities (such as fuel for a cooking stove and/or cabin heater; electricity, water, and garbage disposal often are included in the slip rent), special fees charged by some marinas, boat registration (generally a minor expense), and general living expenses (such as food, clothing, recreation, health care, shore transportation, and so on). If the boat is to be mobile, the operational costs must be added to the above.

Expenses vary greatly, not only with lifestyles, but also with location and type and size of boat. Of course, whether or not the boat is paid for makes a big difference in the size of the monthly bills. Some people spend as much as or more than they did when they lived on land; others spend much less.

In my own case, I have found boat living to be much less expensive than the less satisfying land life I left behind. While many of the expenses have increased over a three-and-a-half-year period, the same increase, if not a larger one, has taken place in the cost of land living. As a sample of what it has cost me, I'll take the most expensive (and thus most recent) year.

Slip rent for the year, including a live-aboard fee, was $500, or an average of $41.67 a month. My homeowner's exemption (which applied to the boat, since it was my principal residence) eliminated my having to pay any property tax. Full-coverage boat insurance was $100 a year, or $8.34 a month. I did all of my own boat maintenance, so the only upkeep expenses were for an annual haul-out and materials and supplies, such as bottom paint. This came to a total of $150 for the year, or $12.50 per month. Fuel for the cooking stove averaged $2 per month. All other utilities were included in the slip rent. Boat registration was $2 per year, or $0.17 per month average. The total for all of the above expenses averaged $64.68 per month. The utility bill alone for many a home on land is more than this.

There have also been times when my expenses were much less — for example, when I did not rent any marina slip and lived in free anchorages, often while cruising. It should also be pointed out that my Westerly Warwick sloop, purchased in 1971, has increased, rather than depreciated, in value. However, whether or not this trend will continue is a matter of speculation.

I know of some people who get by on much less money than I do, and others who spend a great deal more. Even those who must make boat payments have kept the total monthly figures lower than those of many typical arrangements for renting or buying apartments or houses. The cost of boat living roughly parallels that of mobile-home living.

The live-aboard life, to be sure, is a compromise. One friend with a philosophical bent put it this way: "We are only so long for this world, and it is up to each individual to decide how he or she is going to use time, space, and matter, for once time is gone, space and matter don't matter."

3 WHAT TO LOOK FOR IN A BOAT

Two essential features of any boat home are *buoyancy* and *livability*. In addition, the boat must be suitable for whatever boating is planned for her; this may range from none all the way up to world-cruising. This quality can be called *performance*. As a general rule, sacrifices in accommodations must be made in order to have greater performance. This will become clearer when we look at the different types of boat homes, but first let's take a closer look at these characteristics.

Buoyancy

The boat not only must float, but also must remain floating under all conditions she is likely to encounter. The term *buoyancy* covers this quality.

The first barrier against sinking generally is a waterproof shell. For example, consider a dishpan, which has a high degree of buoyancy as long as water does not get inside as a result of leaking, capsizing, or swamping. One way to improve buoyancy would be to change the shape of the dishpan or to add weight (ballast) selectively to the bottom of it, so that it would be less likely to capsize.

A second way to improve buoyancy would be to make the shell into a sealed container. This would eliminate the possibility of sinking from either capsizing or swamping.

The above methods of maintaining buoyancy all depend on the shell remaining waterproof, but if there is one tiny leak below the waterline, it is likely to sink. This is not a quieting thought. So, another improvement might be a pumping system to remove the water from the inside of the dishpan as it enters, but since this is really an emergency system to back up any failure of the primary methods of achieving buoyancy, it will be disregarded for the purposes of the present discussion.

Two methods to achieve greater buoyancy are commonly used on boats, either individually or in combination. One method is to divide the boat hull into watertight sections (open at the top or sealed) so that a leak in any section will not cause the boat to sink. The second method is to fill sections inside the hull with a low-density flotation material that will not absorb water so that the boat will remain afloat, even if she is filled with water.

Livability

The second essential feature of a boat home is livability — the security, comfort, and convenience of the living accommodations. Not only must the interior be considered, but also parts of the exterior, such as cockpits (which may serve as patios and sundecks). Various aspects of livability will be treated throughout the remainder of this book; for now, we will take only a brief look at some of the most important factors.

First, let's look at size. Most people dream of something quite large. But size costs dearly in boats, and most people who turn the dream into a reality have to settle for much less.

One way to look at size is by the length overall (LOA) of the boat, which is measured without including boomkins and bowsprits. As a general rule, each foot of boat length will cost more than the previous one. For example, take a 20-foot sailboat that costs about $5,000 and a 40-footer of comparable quality that is priced at $40,000. This comes to $250 a foot for the 20-footer and $1,000 a foot for the 40-footer, or four times as much per foot. However, if we look at size in terms of the area of interior accommodations, this particular 40-footer actually is more than four times as large as the 20-footer: the larger length overall allows both wider beam and greater cabin height.

Shape also enters the picture. A box shape, either square or rectangular, offers the greatest total interior volume, but unless you are willing to make sacrifices in performance (see following section), this shape is not practical.

In most boats, interior space is at a premium, and fitting in the furnishings (tables, berths, galley components, etc.), choosing their sizes, shapes, and arrangement, becomes a juggling act. The basic components of the interior are galley, dinette, seating, berths, and space for toilet compartment, storage, and moving about. While opinions vary as to what is the best arrangement for any given size and type of boat, it is desirable to have everything arranged for comfort and convenience, keeping in mind the number of people who are going to live aboard. This means trying not to fit in too many things, because open space is important, too.

In spite of advertising claims, most stock boats are not designed with permanent living arrangements. For example, the current manufacturing ideal seems to be to cram as many berths into a boat as possible, regardless of whether any of them is really satisfactory. It is much better to have a good berth for each person (or double berth for couples, if preferred) than a surplus of unsatisfactory ones. Guest berths should be considered only after the residents have been well provided for.

Many stock boats have components serving multiple functions, such as dinettes that convert to berths and berths that are also used as settees. This should be avoided. The sleeping berths should be separate from the general living arrangement, and in a separate compartment or compartments if possible. Converting a dinette into a berth each night, then changing it back to a dinette each morning, is inconvenient, to say the least.

To complicate the matter, considerable space must be allotted for storage. In a functional boat, this means space for boating gear, clothing, items for daily living, and other possessions. Most boats will easily handle the necessities, but the extras generally have to be kept to a minimum.

If possible, everything in the boat should be full size, including furnishings and appliances. However, some compromises almost always will have to be made. Remember that more space for one thing means less space for something else.

If a boat is to be a home, she must be comfortable. This means berths that are big enough, with good mattresses. The settees should be the right height, depth, and softness. The dinette table should be the right height. This concept applies to all aspects of the boat. Accommodations that may be tolerable for occasional overnighting, which most stock boats are designed for, can be quite unsatisfactory for daily living.

Equipment is another important consideration (see Chapter 4). Many modern appliances are available for marine use, but there are generally limitations on both the number and size that can be used.

Ventilation and insulation are often overlooked. One thin layer of fiberglass, for example, offers little insulation, yet it's all you get with many stock boats.

What is the minimum livability required? There is no one answer. Living requirements are highly individual. What is acceptable to one person may be intolerable to another. For example, one prevalent view is that a 30-foot boat is the minimum size needed for a couple. But what I have seen in practice does not bear this out. I know of couples who apparently live successfully in boats smaller than this, and other couples who live unsuccessfully in much larger boats.

A look at one factor, headroom, will further illustrate this point. I feel that standing headroom (a minimum of six feet) is essential, at least in the galley area and preferably throughout. Yet, there are many people who get along without it.

At its price, the Westerly Warwick was a good choice for me. She has a lot of room for her small size, including standing headroom, enclosed head, ample berths, and a dinette. I feel, however, that my boat would be much too small for more than one person.

While cost considerations will probably place the boat well below the dream level, it seems advisable that the accommodations at least be a bit above the minimum that you consider tolerable.

Boat performance

Buoyancy and livability are the essentials, but you may also want performance (the ability of the floating home to function as a boat, to move from place to place in the water by means of sails or engine).

A first thing to note is that as the boat moves into less protected waters, a higher degree of buoyancy or seaworthiness is required.

If overall length and breadth (beam) remain constant, increased performance requires sacrifice of space that could otherwise be used for living accommodations, both because of shape (a pointed bow reduces interior volume) and because space is needed for propelling and handling the boat.

Other factors that help make up performance (besides seaworthiness) include speed, ease of handling, seakindliness, and economy of operation and maintenance.

When selecting a boat, keep in mind her intended use. Some of the possible uses are racing (although beyond the beer-can level, racing generally is incompatible with living aboard), cruising, fishing, and chartering (see Chapter 11).

Since performance costs money, the amount of performance needed should be estimated carefully. You should have enough for intended use, plus a healthy safety margin, but anything beyond this is generally uneconomical. A world-cruising sailboat permanently moored in well-protected waters is an example of excessive performance potential. By the same token, an ordinary houseboat cannot make ocean passages, a few stunts notwithstanding.

Ease of maintenance

High on the list of requirements is ease of maintenance. There's no such thing as a no-maintenance boat, but some require much less than others. (The how-to aspects of this subject are covered in Chapter 12.) Ease of maintenance depends not only on design and construction, but also on the kind and quality of materials used.

Construction materials

Both design and construction are related to some degree to the construction materials used. Most boats are made of a number of different materials, but generally a boat is classified by the primary hull material. The most common materials are fiberglass, wood, steel, aluminum, and ferrocement (including variations), or a combination of wood (generally plywood, either sheets or cold-molded) sheathed with fiberglass. Space does not permit detailed treatment here of design and construction using these materials; in fact, an entire book can hardly do justice to even one of these materials. However, some knowledge of design and construction is needed for intelligent selection of a boat, so a recommended reading list is included in the Appendix. If you have decided definitely on a certain material, then it might not be necessary to read about the other materials, but be sure to read everything you can find on the material you have chosen.

Fiberglass. Most boats manufactured today are made of fiberglass, and this category offers the largest selection of boats. Fiberglass has a number of advantages over other construction materials, and I prefer it because it is easy to maintain, but there are disadvantages, too.

Advantages include durability, value, comparative ease of maintenance and repair, and freedom from corrosion and teredo-worm problems. A high-quality, well-designed fiberglass boat is strong and damage-resistant, and should last for many years. Some of the earliest stock fiberglass boats, built in the 1940s, still have hulls in good condition. Fiberglass boats have a high resale value, which is an advan-

tage when you sell, but a disadvantage when you buy. Since few scantlings (frames, stringers, bulkheads and other members used for rein-
forcing the hull, deck, and cabin structures) are required, it is possible
to have greater interior dimensions than with a wooden boat of the
same exterior size. Maintenance for a fiberglass boat generally costs
less (or is easier to do if you do it yourself) than for boats of wood or
steel. Fiberglass boats *do* require maintenance, but much of it is cosmetic. Neglect seldom causes serious damage, as it often can with
wood and steel boats.

Disadvantages of fiberglass include sweating and poor sound insulation. These problems can be partially alleviated by adding insulation materials, but it's difficult to equal the dryness and the solid
sound of a good wooden boat.

It should also be mentioned that thousands of inadequate fiberglass boats have been sold. Many are even unsafe. Despite new federal safety standards, inadequate boats are still being turned out.
Every would-be purchaser of a fiberglass boat should arm himself
with enough knowledge about fiberglass boat design and construction to avoid getting stuck with a "lemon," a "clunker," or whatever
you want to call one of these boats. Common structural weaknesses
include: poor methods and materials of hull construction; inadequate hull-to-deck bonding methods and keel-to-hull connections;
weaknesses in rudder posts and assemblies; and improper installation
of windows, ports, and fittings.

Wood. Stock wooden boats, once the mainstay of the boating in-
dustry, are becoming both rare and expensive. Good used wood
boats are also becoming scarce, and they demand a premium price.
Some are sold as "classics." Rotten wood boats and those with
teredo worms are cheap and seldom, if ever, worth the price. Plywood boats sheathed in fiberglass are treated in a separate section
below.

Probably more is known about wooden boats than those constructed of other materials. They've been around since before recorded
history. Perhaps the main advantage of this material is that it is considered to be "warm and natural," as opposed to, say, fiberglass,
which is considered to be "cold" and is a synthetic. Because of the
high cost, the difficulty in getting suitable wood, and the large
amount of skilled labor required, not many wooden boats are being
manufactured today — a definite disadvantage if you want to buy
one. Wooden boats also require considerable maintenance if teredo-
worm and dry-rot problems are to be prevented.

Steel. If properly constructed, boats made of steel are strong, but they generally are expensive and are built only on a custom basis. They require regular maintenance if rust and electrolysis problems are to be prevented. Even with these limitations, some people have found them to be acceptable.

Aluminum. Aluminum is used rarely in stock boats. It offers a number of advantages for racing sailboats, such as its light weight, but cost and construction difficulties generally preclude its use, other than perhaps in houseboats, where flat sections and riveted construction are practical.

Ferrocement. Ferrocement has been hailed widely as the boat-building material of the future. As far as manufacturing is concerned, it remains in the future: only a very small percentage of manufactured boats are made of ferrocement. Ferrocement seems popular with home builders (see Chapter 7). I've seen some successes here, and many failures. Still, this is one route to a boat home, and it should certainly be given consideration.

Plywood sheathed in fiberglass. A few boats have been manufactured with sheets of plywood or cold-molded construction sheathed with fiberglass. While only a few boats suitable for living aboard are produced on a regular basis, there are a number of firms that do this type of boatbuilding on a custom or semicustom basis. This method is popular for backyard construction of boats, especially trimarans; and for "ground up" building, I feel that it is one of the most practical approaches. However, some problems ought to be mentioned: it is extremely difficult to achieve a good bond between the wood and fiberglass, dry rot is common, and worms can enter the wood through a small damaged area. Unless only the outside is sheathed, there is the danger of trapping moisture. By no means are all of the advantages of fiberglass gained by merely sheathing wood with fiberglass.

Types of boats

While certain boats seem to fall into definite categories, others are more difficult to place. Since all boat homes must have buoyancy and livability, I will classify them according to performance as follows: (1) floating houses, which are not intended for boating at all, (2) houseboats, which have limited performance, and (3) power and sailboats, including combinations of the two, which can have a great performance.

Figure 3. *This floating home features 4 bedrooms, 2½ baths, and central heating and air conditioning. (Courtesy Sea View Floating Homes.)*

Floating houses (also called "floating homes," "boat houses," and "dock houses"). These are essentially houses built on floats or rafts and intended for more or less permanent mooring. They often look much like land houses. In most cases, they have no means of self-propulsion, and if they are to be moved to another location, they must be towed. Some have provisions for attaching an outboard, but this provides only slow and limited movement.

Floating houses (most of which are built by their owners) have long been popular in a few isolated sections of the United States (for instance: along the Mississippi River; on the inland waterways of Florida, Alabama, and Louisiana; in the California Delta area; and in Sausalito, California), but only recently has their spreading popularity prompted manufacturers and building contractors to take an interest. Presently there is something of a boom demand for this type of housing.

Floating houses generally offer the greatest livability at the lowest cost, but only at the sacrifice of all performance. It is not uncommon to see a boat moored to a floating house, and this combination certainly has a lot going for it: the floating house is used for living and the boat for boating.

Except for the fact that they can be moved to a new location without too much difficulty, floating houses are similar to houses built out over the water on pilings, or houses at the water's edge. In the larger and more elaborate floating houses, most of the comforts and conveniences typical of a modern land house are possible. An important advantage is that mooring is generally much less expensive than purchasing a piece of waterfront property. In many areas, the floating house also offers significant tax advantages.

Houseboats. These generally have more streamlined underwater shapes and cabin houses, outboard or inboard power, and a higher price tag for comparable size than floating houses. However, of the functional boats, houseboats tend to be lower-priced than other types of craft. Houseboats are ideally suited for living and cruising in well-protected waters.

Houseboats are available with pontoon-type and regular hulls, in a variety of bottom designs. Most houseboats have shallow draft.

If a houseboat has enough functional boating ability for your needs and the waters where you intend to use her, you may save quite a bit of money by buying this type of craft rather than a power cruiser or sailboat. If you plan to use her for extensive cruising, however, be sure that you consider operating costs.

Figure 4. *The Executive 48 fiberglass houseboat. (Courtesy Holiday Mansion.)*

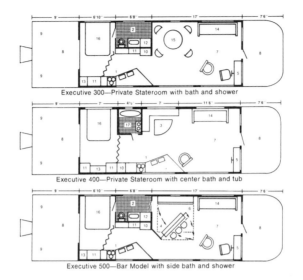

Executive 300—Private Stateroom with bath and shower

Executive 400—Private Stateroom with center bath and tub

Executive 500—Bar Model with side bath and shower

Figure 5. *The Executive 48 houseboat is available with 3 different floor plans. (Courtesy Holiday Mansion.)*

Figure 6. *The 40-foot Royal Capri houseboat is available with accommodations for sleeping 6 or 10. (Courtesy Kayot Marine Division.)*

Power, sail, and combination boats. Sailboats and power cruisers come in a great range of performing ability, starting somewhat above houseboats and going all the way up to oceangoing boats. While more seaworthy than houseboats, they usually have less living space and higher price tags.

The first decision to make here is whether to buy power, sail, or a combination of the two. While I've known a few people who were undecided between power and sail, most are firmly set one way or the other. While most sailboats have auxiliary power, these are generally still classified as sailboats. Boats with less than full-sail ability and good power capabilities are called motorsailers, although it is almost impossible to draw the exact line between a motorsailer and an auxiliary-powered sailboat.

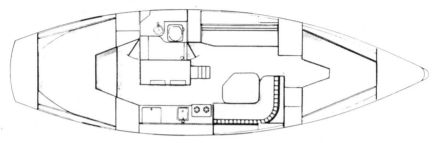

Figure 7. Above: *Accommodation plan for Coronado's 35-foot tri-cabin sailboat — ideal for living aboard.* Below: *The Coronado 35's aft cabin, looking toward walk-through passageway. (Courtesy Coronado Yachts.)*

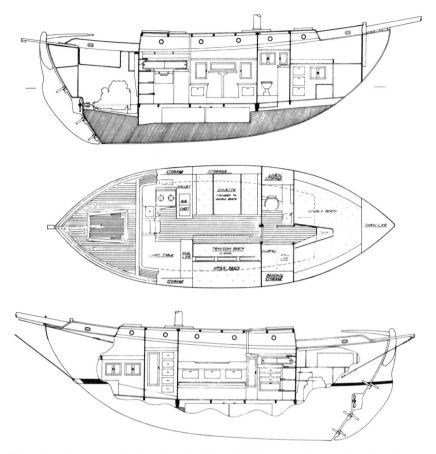

Figure 8. *Accommodation plans for Westsail 32, a popular live-aboard and world-cruising sailboat. (Courtesy Westsail Corp.)*

As a general rule, a powerboat will have more interior living space than a sailboat of equal length, because sailboats almost always have finer hull lines.

Many different types of powerboats have been used as boat homes. One point to keep in mind is that speed costs money. This is especially important if extensive cruising is planned. Displacement hulls are slower, but they have better fuel economy than the faster planing hulls. Although the arguments can go on endlessly, I feel that diesel engines are well worth the generally higher initial cost, as compared

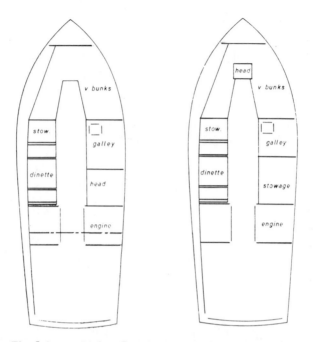

Figure 9. *The Johnson 32-foot Prowler is available with 2 different accommo-dation plans. (Courtesy Forest E. Johnson & Sons, Inc.)*

Figure 10. *The Gulfstar 36 trawler yacht Mark II has go-anywhere capabilities. (Courtesy Gulfstar, Inc.)*

to gas engines, because diesel offers greater safety and economy. In any case, I believe that one should carefully consider the dangers of a gasoline engine and weigh these against the possible savings in the initial purchase.

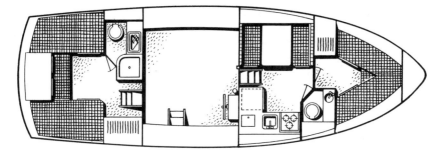

Figure 11. *The Gulfstar 36 trawler yacht has an efficient layout. (Courtesy Gulfstar, Inc.)*

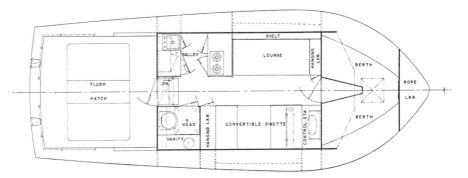

Figure 12. *The Luhrs 32-foot flybridge sedan cruiser offers several accommodation plans, of which one is shown above. (Courtesy Luhrs Company.)*

Opinions vary on the relative costs of operating power- and sailboats. Much depends on the particular boat and her use.

One can also choose among hull types. While most boats are monohulls (single hull), there are also catamarans (two hulls) and trimarans (generally with a main center hull and two floats or smaller outer hulls). Catamarans and trimarans are popular build-it-yourself boats for living aboard. Trimarans in particular deserve more discussion.

Trimarans are often said to have more interior space than monohulls of the same length. This may be true as far as total interior volume is concerned, but whether they provide more practical and usable space is often another matter. Having built and used a 30-foot trimaran, I feel that the interior accommodations of my 21½-foot Westerly monohull are much better. To be sure, the trimaran had large double berths out over the cross-arms, but these had only a couple of feet overhead, making sitting up on the berths impossible, not to mention the difficulty of crawling into them. To get to the forward cabin, where the toilet compartment was located, it was necessary to crawl under the forward cross-arm. My little Westerly allows sitting headroom in all three of her single berths, and there is 5 feet 10 inches of headroom (no crawling!) to get to the toilet compartment.

Another problem with trimarans, and often with catamarans, is their extremely wide beam, which can make it difficult to find docking space at marinas.

I found my trimaran to be fast and fun to sail on certain points; on others, she made good sideways about as well as she did forward.

One of the reasons for the popularity of the trimaran as a home is that she is fairly easy for amateurs to build. This can be a plus when buying, since used, amateur-built trimarans can often be purchased inexpensively.

My own personal preference for a boat home is a fiberglass mono-hull sailboat, for all of the various reasons outlined in this chapter.

4 INTERIOR LAYOUTS, FURNISHINGS, AND DECOR

While it is common practice to design floating homes around the desired accommodations with a minimum of limitations, functional boats are designed as boats first, before the accommodations are fitted in. Many amateur boatbuilders fail to understand this, and they add upward and outward far beyond the designer's plans, often producing disastrous results, such as boats that float on their sides or upside-down. In other words, a given boat design and size is limited to a certain interior shape and amount of space. Of course, it may be possible to increase the cabin size without significantly reducing the performance and safety of the vessel, but such design changes are best left to professionals.

Even with this limitation, however, many different living arrangements are possible within a given hull size and form. Much can be done with interior layouts, furnishings, and decor.

Interior layouts

The interior layout of a floating home can be much like that of a house or apartment of equal size, and for this type of boat I think it is best to think in terms of a house. The arrangements of houseboats are often similar to those of trailer homes. Power cruisers and sailboats have additional limitations that must be taken into consideration.

Most manufacturers will provide drawings of their boats' accommodations to prospective buyers. These drawings may be confusing until you've had a chance to compare them with the actual boats. Visiting boats at boat shows and in dealers' showrooms is a good way to familiarize yourself with accommodations. But don't decide in haste. Try to gain perspective for relating drawings to the inside of

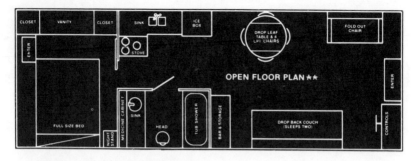

Figure 13. *The 43-foot Drifter houseboat has a spacious floor plan. (Courtesy House Boating Corporation of America.)*

the boat, so that you later can form a good idea of the interior of a boat from the drawings alone.

In planning an interior layout, be sure you again take into account what kind of boating you plan to do. A need for seaworthiness will limit the number of practical interior arrangements. What might be fully functional at dockside could well be hopeless at sea. For protected inland waters, a trailer-type interior may be satisfactory, but for offshore boating this could be impractical and even dangerous. Special boat furniture has been developed for just this reason.

Some open space is required for walking and moving about. It seems to me that many stock boats have too many things fitted in and not enough open space. It's important to be able to move about freely without having to squeeze through narrow aisles and doorways. Check this out thoroughly.

Another variable is the number, size, and arrangement of separate compartments. In a floating house, these are generally called rooms, and they can be thought of as such. In a boat, the bedroom becomes the stateroom; the living room, the saloon; and so on.

It is best to have sleeping quarters for all residents in one or more compartments separate from the main saloon. In small boats, the typical arrangement is one separated sleeping compartment forward, often with a V-berth. In larger boats, starting at around 35 or 36 feet in power cruisers and sailboats, it is practical to have an aft cabin, in addition to the forward cabin. If a walk-through passageway is possible, then one does not have to go above, through a center cockpit, to get from the saloon to the aft cabin. In any case, it is preferable to have the sleeping compartments separated by doors rather than by curtains. The more boxlike shape of a houseboat allows a larger variety of arrangements, but the separate sleeping-room concept still applies.

Another important consideration is the convenience and privacy of the bathroom, toilet room, or head. I recommend at least one separate compartment with a solid swinging door. Less satisfactory arrangements involve sliding or accordion doors that, to close off the head, separate the forward cabin from the saloon.

In tri-cabin boats, such as those with a center cockpit, two head compartments — one near each sleeping compartment — may be desirable. However, it should be remembered that duplicate components can mean additional breakdowns, so the need for two heads should be considered carefully, especially if offshore boating is foreseen. Backup systems for equipment and gear vital to the safety of the craft are another matter, of course, but the head does not fit into this category.

Designers and manufacturers seem to have different ideas about how much space should be devoted to closets and hanging lockers. Make sure that these are adequate for your needs. A separate compartment with a solid sliding or hinged door is preferable.

In most small power cruisers, sailboats, and houseboats, the main living area, including the kitchen or galley, is generally a one-room (or cabin) efficiency arrangement, although the kitchen or galley is often partially separated from the dining and seating area. In boats with deckhouses, the main living area may be divided into two different cabin-floor levels. There are a number of variations, such as main seating arrangement in deckhouse and dinette and galley in forward compartment, or galley only in forward section and both seating and dinette areas in deckhouse. The latter has the advantage of providing a better view during dining.

Several arrangements are common in boats with a single saloon area. For example, the galley can be located along one side of the cabin or aft, in an L-shape or a U-shape. The aft galley is often recommended for cruising boats because ventilation is easier there, and it is convenient to both the cockpit and saloon areas. However, many people have found a side galley satisfactory, although additional vents may be needed. Some stock boats are available with a choice of several interior layouts, and one basic difference is often the location of the galley. Personally, I would prefer having the galley by the companionway. In my Westerly, however, it would be impractical, as it would preclude berths that extend under the cockpit seats. The galley in the Westerly is forward in the main cabin, with the stove on the port side and the sink and icebox on the star-board side. This arrangement is satisfactory for me, but I'm the type of person who eats to live rather than one who lives to eat.

A long settee similar to a sofa is typical seating on a boat. Ideally, this is in addition to and separate from table seating.

There are several popular table arrangements on production boats. These include: a table extending out from one side of the boat with a settee on each side; L- and U-shaped arrangements; and the sea table, which is a table located near the centerline with settees or berths being used for seating.

Although there are many different opinions about layouts, there are also some basic considerations:

(1) Be sure that the space allotted for various purposes is adequate.

(2) The arrangement of the central saloon is especially important, because it is used for general living, dining, playing, and lounging.

(3) The less "doubling," the better. Whenever possible, avoid ar-rangements that involve conversion from one purpose to another.

Furnishings

Furnishings here include both furniture and appliances. In float-ing houses, it is common practice to use the same type, and usually the same size, furniture and appliances used in land houses. While some of the same furniture and appliances are used aboard house-boats, built-in furnishings and appliances of reduced size, like those used in travel trailers, are more common. Power cruisers and sail-boats generally have almost everything built in, and appliances and equipment are almost always compromises of land-based versions. Built-in furniture can be fitted to odd shapes. If space permits, free-standing furniture can be used, but in functional boats it's gen-erally necessary to secure it with straps or cables.

As space becomes more critical, compromises become more im-portant. The settees should be the right height and depth, have a backrest, and have the right amount and placement of padding. Try them out. If they feel wrong immediately, they will probably feel worse after a year. Before discarding a boat solely on this account, however, consider modifications (see Chapter 8).

The importance of having full headroom was stressed in Chapter 3. Footroom is equally important. I've seen stock boats that have dinettes that supposedly seat four, but they have leg space for only two pairs of legs. The boat's dining area should at least have space for the residents, but comfortable seating for a reasonable number of guests should also be considered.

Check the traffic flow. Are the furnishings arranged so they can be used conveniently by all? Try to avoid such things as aisles so narrow that two people can't pass each other, tables where everyone has to get up to let one person out, and tables that, when in use, completely block the aisle from one section of the boat to another.

Following are some important points:

Berths. The sleeping berths that will be used regularly should be full length. I think that at least a few inches, and preferably six or eight inches extra (i.e., longer than the height of the sleeper), is a good idea. While many stock boats come with two- or three-inch mattresses, five or six inches makes more sense for permanent boat living. Cloth-covered mattresses generally are more comfortable than plastic ones, especially in hot weather.

Tables. A table should be the right height for the seating, large enough, sturdy, and easy to keep clean. Typical problems are tables that wobble and brackets and legs that are inadequate. In some cases, legs and braces hinder comfortable seating.

Galleys. Counters should be the right height and there should be adequate working space. Many stock boats have sinks that are too small to be practical. From experience I have found stainless-steel sinks to be superior to those of molded fiberglass, which wear and are difficult to keep clean. Cabinets, racks, and drawers should be arranged conveniently.

Refrigerators and freezers. With shore power, a 110-volt, alternating-current unit is generally the least expensive and most practical for refrigerators. However, this presents difficulties during boating. A number of refrigeration units can be switched back and forth between alternating-current shore power or direct-current battery power. For those who plan on boating, I feel that this is the best solution, assuming that the boat's engine has the charging capacity to operate the refrigerator with a reasonably short period of operation — say, half an hour or less per day. If the boat's engine will not handle this, an auxiliary generating unit is another possibility. However, my personal opinion is that it would be better to make do with a simple icebox or without any means of refrigeration. This applies especially to those who are on a tight budget or who do not like to have to bother with mechanical repairs and maintenance.

Another possibility you may want to consider for a refrigeration

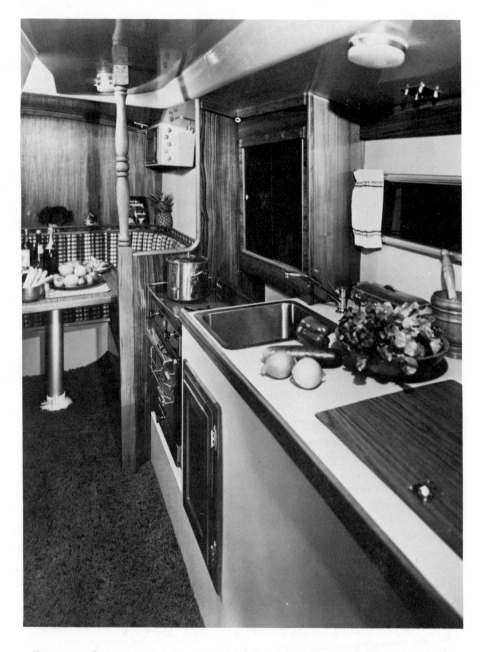

Figure 14. *Galley and dinette of 35-foot Coronado sailboat. (Courtesy Coronado Yachts.)*

Figure 15. *This 4.3 cu. ft. icebox is available with components that convert it to a refrigerator or freezer. (Courtesy Marine Development Corporation.)*

unit is a "holdover plate," which can run off a compressor powered by the main engine or a separate power unit. There are also absorption-type units. These require a small, continuous flame. There are models that burn either kerosene or propane. For safety reasons, I would not have this type of unit on my boat. However, judging from their popularity, many people feel otherwise. If a choice is to be made between kerosene and propane, kerosene is preferable, because the fumes are lighter than air, making it safer than propane, which is heavier than air and can collect in the bilge.

Marine refrigerators and freezers are available at marine stores and from mail-order houses.

Cabin heat. For comfortable living in cold weather, a heating system is a must. With good insulation, a little heat will go a long way in the snug interior of a boat. In a modern floating home, heating

Figure 16. *This unique stove offers the advantages of both a cabin heater and a fireplace. (Courtesy Ratelco, Inc.)*

Figure 17. *The Shipmate cabin heater is made of stainless steel, burns kerosene, and is safety vented. (Courtesy Richmond Ring Co.)*

requirements are similar to those of a land dwelling of the same size and with the same amount of insulation.

With shore power, small electric heaters with fans are often used. Many people favor wood-, charcoal-, or coke-burning heaters. A number of types and sizes are available. Some are wall-mounted and others stand on a floor or counter, such as cast-iron potbellied stoves. These require a chimney pipe. An important advantage of a cabin heater is that it tends to draw moisture out of the cabin. I prefer a wood-burning stove for cold climates. It provides a dry, cozy cabin. In a small boat, only a limited quantity of wood is required, and this is available in most areas. The ashes must be removed from these stoves from time to time, but the type of heat provided is well worth the trouble. Safety, of course, must be considered with all heaters, but it is especially important with these solid-fuel units. They can be quite safe, however, provided that: a stove specially designed for boat use is properly installed, reasonable care is taken when it is op- erated, and there is no gasoline or propane anywhere aboard the boat.

Other possibilities are kerosene and diesel heaters. One disadvan- tage is that they consume oxygen and give off carbon monoxide, so adequate ventilation must be provided. Still another type of heater sometimes used is an alcohol catalytic model.

Propane heaters are often used, but I feel that even if they are vented outward, they are not safe, especially on cruising boats. These heaters may be acceptable, however, for houseboats and floating homes.

Fireplaces similar to those used in land houses are often installed in floating homes. Many floating homes have shore connections to natural gas, making standard house furnaces practical.

Generators. Two common generator systems are used: a genera- tor run off the boat's engine and a separate generator. A number of separate gasoline and diesel generators are now on the market. With- out the convenience of shore power, it is practical to have equip- ment such as televisions, stereo sets, broilers, etc., that will operate on direct current (DC), the type supplied by batteries. Direct cur- rent from batteries can be changed to alternating current (AC), the current commonly used in homes ashore, by means of an inverter, but the lower-voltage DC generally is safer. Marine stores and mail- order outlets sell appliances that can operate on either AC line cur- rent or DC battery power. Usually, the appliance itself operates on either one or the other and the power conversions are made between the source and the appliance by an inverter that is often built right into the appliance so that a change from one power source to the other is made by a simple click of a switch.

Pressure water systems. A pressure water system eliminates the need for operating a mechanical pump by hand or foot. Modern boats frequently are equipped with electric pressure systems, which may be switch- or faucet-activated. Another possibility is a gravity

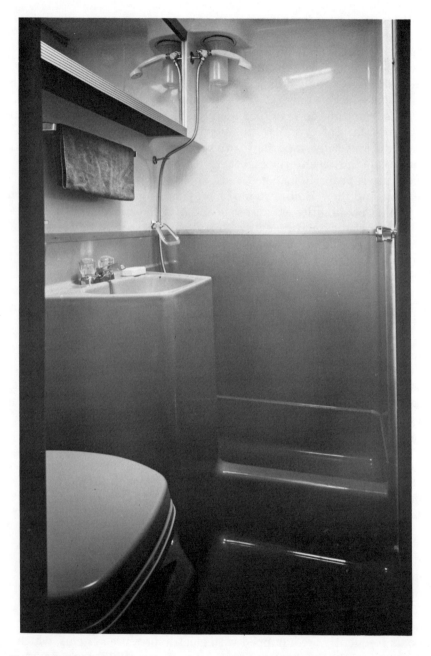

Figure 18. *Head layout on Kayot 35- and 40-foot houseboats. (Courtesy Kayot Marine Division.)*

pressure system. Water is pumped (often from the regular water tanks by means of a rotary hand pump) to a gravity tank, which is at a higher level than the water tap. This arrangement can be combined with a solar system for heating the water by placing the gravity tank outside on the deck or cabin top, and painting it black.

Hot water. Hot water can make life more comfortable and convenient. The most primitive and simplest system is to heat a pot of water on the stove. With shore electrical power, a small electric water heater is relatively inexpensive, and it has important safety advantages over those requiring a flame. Without shore power, an internal coil through which hot engine water passes is perhaps the best bet. While the efficiency of systems varies, the average engine-running time to heat eight or 10 gallons of water to 160 degrees is about 15 minutes.

Without engine operation or shore power, kerosene- and diesel-fired water heaters can be used. Another possibility is a propane model, but it requires an air intake and an exhaust vent and it is more dangerous. Some insurance companies charge higher premiums if you have propane-operated equipment, and their premiums are based on experience.

Showers. When living at a marina with shore facilities, many people do without shower facilities, especially on the smaller boats. Unless the shower is properly vented, it can bring a great deal of moisture into the boat. Besides the shower head, a stall, floor grating, and sump generally are required for the installation. When the boat is not connected to a shore water supply, a "telephone"-type shower head with hot and cold knobs or push-button on/off controls with a flexible hose will help conserve water, but even with this arrangement, a shower will require at least a couple of gallons of water. The water collected in the sump is discharged by a pumping system overboard or into a holding tank.

Cooking stoves. The basic choices for stoves are those that burn alcohol, bottled gas (propane, butane, or a mixture of the two), compressed natural gas (CNG), kerosene, diesel fuel, and wood. A wide variety of models, from one-burner affairs to those with a number of burners and ovens, are available for each of these fuels. Another possibility is an electric stove. Each of these choices has advantages and disadvantages, and it's important to consider them carefully. One consideration that applies to all types of stoves is the availability of parts. Check on this before you buy, because it is just about impossible to get replacement parts for some brands and models.

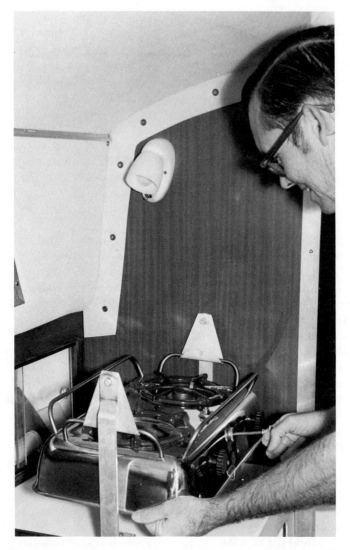

Figure 19. *A pressure-feed alcohol stove always requires pumping before it is lighted. (Photo by author.)*

Alcohol is considered to be a safe fuel, although flare-ups are reported to be a danger. I have been using a two-burner Homestrand alcohol stove, mounted on gimbals, for nearly four years, and I have not experienced any serious problems with flare-ups. The stove has been completely reliable, requiring no repairs. The only maintenance has been simple cleaning.

The main disadvantages of alcohol are the comparatively high cost of the fuel, the low heat output, and the pumping required to build up pressure in the tank (for pressure models; some work by gravity and do not require pumping). An important advantage is that alcohol fires can be extinguished with water.

Propane and butane stoves are probably the most convenient. To light them, you simply open the fuel valve and light the burners with a match. Also, they put out much more heat than alcohol stoves. The main disadvantage is the high risk of explosion, because of the heavier-than-air propane. In spite of this danger, this is a popular fuel. If you do use it, leave the installation to experts.

I have had no personal experience with compressed natural gas. Gas Systems, Inc., 6400 Marina Drive, Long Beach, California 90803, supplied me with the following information: Compressed natural gas is now available on fuel docks in all marinas throughout California, and it soon will be available in other areas. (*Author's note: They did not specify the areas.*) A complete line of natural-gas appliances — including cooktop stoves, ranges with ovens, and refrigerators — is available from Gas Systems. Unlike propane or butane, CNG is lighter than air, and should a leak in the fuel system occur, the CNG will not settle in the bilge. The gas, which is odorized, will rise to the top of a cabin and seek a way out of the boat. CNG is easily lighted and does not have to be primed. Cylinders of CNG are initially purchased on a permanent lease basis, as required by federal law, so that they can be properly inspected, tested, and refilled by Gas Systems. Empty cylinders can be exchanged for full ones at a fuel dock or shipped anywhere for a small service charge. For more information, write to the firm at the above address.

Kerosene is my personal first choice for a stove fuel. Considering everything, it is one of the safest fuels to use aboard boats, and it burns at a higher temperature than alcohol. Kerosene is generally less expensive than alcohol. While both alcohol and kerosene are readily available in all parts of the United States, kerosene is much easier to get than alcohol in many parts of the world, an important consideration for those planning world cruises. On the minus side, kerosene stoves require pumping and are sometimes difficult to light. Most kerosene stoves use a small amount of alcohol at each lighting for priming the burner.

Diesel oil is very popular as a stove fuel on fishing boats that operate in cold climates. If the boat also has a diesel engine, only one type of fuel need be carried for both the engine and stove.

Wood-burning stoves are cozy in colder climates, but they add too much heat to the cabin in warm weather, and they are much less convenient to operate than most other types. While wood stoves are generally free from breakdowns, an important consideration for people on a tight budget, wood can be expensive if you have to purchase it, and stowage is limited in a small boat.

At first thought, electric stoves might seem ideal for use at dockside with shore power. However, they draw a lot of current, and many marinas are not equipped to handle this load.

Operating electric stoves off the boat's generating and battery system is generally impractical, as it requires either a lot of engine-running time or a hefty generating plant. Electric cooking equipment does offer many important safety advantages, but these are often offset by careless handling and installation of the equipment. For example, a small hot plate sitting loose on a table can be thrown to the cabin sole by the wake of a passing motorboat and possibly start a fire.

Lockers and storage. With limited interior space, storage becomes a considerable problem. The main types of storage are lockers, cabinets, drawers, and bins. Make sure that there will be a place for everything, including boating gear, clothing, personal belongings, and food. In many cases, boats without adequate storage space can be improved by simple modifications (see Chapter 8), such as the addition of special racks and shelves.

It is difficult to give any meaningful estimate of the minimum amount of storage space required per person, as everyone seems to have different requirements. Aboard the *Sea Puppy*, I find barely enough space to store my own things, and I use all the berths except the one I sleep on as storage bins. If all the berths were occupied, I might have problems.

Storage at dockside in protected waters is relatively simple, compared to being underway (see Chapter 10). At sea, fiddles are necessary to keep things from sliding off shelves and tables, and drawers should be self-locking so that the motion of the boat will not open them.

Sewage Disposal. An on-board toilet that can be used at the mooring is highly desirable, if not essential. The two methods most widely advocated for private sewage disposal are treatment of raw sewage before discharge, such as maceration, and use of holding tanks and shore-side facilities for pumping them out. Maceration requires electric power daily, and it is being debated seriously whether or not the discharge into the water is adequately treated to prevent pollution. Although the laws are still confusing, in the United States the choice generally is limited to a holding tank or a direct connection to a shore sewage system. If you want to go boating, the latter is unsuitable, as the system would have to be disconnected. However, the direct connection to a shore system is ideal for permanently moored floating homes. Holding tanks must have a large capacity (at least 20 gallons) to be practical. Recirculating systems can increase the time between pump-outs at a disposal station.

A direct-discharge toilet should not be the only facility in the boat (assuming that this will cause significant pollution — some experts do not think so), because it is next to impossible to keep from using it. Imagine the temptation in the middle of a cold night with shore facilities some distance away.

Since laws vary, and in many areas there are few or no pump-out stations, and in others, fees are charged for each pump-out, it is best to study the laws carefully and find out what others in your area do about this problem before you decide on a system.

Ventilation and screening. Air should be able to circulate freely throughout all parts of the boat, including lockers and storage compartments. Ventilation is important not only for human comfort, but also for reduction of dampness and condensation, which can lead to mold, mildew, and — in the case of wood — dry rot.

Ventilation typically provided is by hatches, vents (generally designed to keep rain and spray water out while letting air pass either in or out), and opening ports or windows. Make sure that it is possible to ventilate the boat properly, even in rainy weather. Also, the ventilation should be adjustable.

Screening is important. Stock boats rarely are equipped with screening, but many people add their own (see Chapter 8).

Other possibilities for improving interior comfort include electric fans, air conditioners, and refrigeration units.

Lighting. Those who want to keep life as simple as possible use kerosene lights in order to do without electricity. Battery or shore power is typical of modern boats. Proper insulation and grounding are essential, however (see Appendix for books devoted to this subject). Here are a few basic requirements for electric lighting:

(1) Light fixtures, wiring, and components should be of marine quality.

(2) Lights should be located for specific jobs, such as for lighting the galley or for reading in bed.

(3) Plug outlets should be placed strategically throughout the boat.

There are other points to keep in mind for nonelectric lighting. Propane/butane lanterns and those operated by white gasoline, such as the ones sold for camping use, are generally considered too dangerous for use in boats. Kerosene lamps are commonly used. They are available with wicks and mantles with or without pressure pump systems. In functional boats, gimbals are recommended. Only fireproof lampshades should be used. Smoke bells and asbestos panels may be required to protect woodwork. Pressure kerosene lamps often hum in an annoying manner, and many require alcohol priming to get them going. Lamps and lanterns should be of marine quality.

Toilet rooms. Toilet rooms should offer complete privacy. There should be space for stowage of toilet articles and towels; suitable counter space, shelves, and racks; a hamper for laundry; and room to move around. There should be a sink and a mirror. Full headroom is highly desirable.

Additional information. Boating equipment is a vast subject, and space permits only a brief introduction here. For additional information, see the Appendix. Equipment catalogs and buyers' guides are especially useful.

Decor

Color, lighting, and use of wall space can enhance or diminish the sense of space. A sense of greater space can be achieved by using light colors and carefully placed mirrors. White or off-white surfaces, with varnished hardwood or oiled teak trim, are common.

Colors can create a mood; for example, I find greens cool, whites clean, ivories warm, grays serviceable, blues cold, and oranges and reds disturbing. These effects can be used to good advantage when you select patterns and color schemes for curtains, lampshades, upholstery, and carpets. Many stock boats come in a wide choice of color schemes.

Beyond this, a satisfying decor includes a lot of little things, like having the right pictures on the bulkheads. Those with a creative bent have done some wonderful things with the relatively small spaces in boats. Certainly the decor contributes a great deal toward making a boat a home.

5 LEGAL REQUIREMENTS AND INSURANCE

Laws regarding living in boats and insurance available to boat residents are complex subjects, and space permits only a general introduction. Sources for additional information are included in the Appendix. Also note that legal requirements are subject to revision and updating, so it is important to refer to the most up-to-date sources available.

Registration and documentation

Laws relating to boat registration vary from state to state. In the few states where there are no relevant state laws, the Coast Guard handles registration. In most states the registration fee is paid annually and is quite low. Nonfunctional floating houses generally are registered in the same way as boats. Anyone considering a floating house should carefully check the situation in the state where the floating house is to be moored.

If you make your purchase through a dealer or broker, registration is generally taken care of at the time of the sale. If a boat is purchased from an individual, registration procedures vary from state to state. Boat dealerships generally can supply the necessary information. In some states, the registration is handled by mail or by the motor-vehicle department.

Documentation with the Coast Guard is an alternative to registration with the state for functional boats of five net tons or larger (this is related to carrying capacity rather than the displacement of the craft; for example, a 27-foot Vega sailboat is in this category). For information on eligibility and procedure for documentation, contact the Coast Guard installation in your area, or write to Coast Guard Headquarters, 400 7th St. S.W., Washington, D.C. 20591.

Documentation may offer certain advantages over registration, especially if the boat will cruise to foreign ports. For new boats, the procedure for documentation is generally quite straightforward, but for used boats, especially if there have been a number of different owners, it can become quite complicated.

Operator's licensing

For pleasure and recreational boating, an operator's license is not presently required. However, licensing is required for charter boats. Licenses are issued by the Coast Guard.

Legal requirements

Most of the federal, state, county, and city requirements concern safety and pollution. According to the Federal Boating Safety Act, manufacturers must meet certain minimum safety standards in the construction of boats. Some boats have been recalled by manufacturers for repair of certain defects. However, judging by the displays at some recent boat shows, the Boating Safety Act has done little to improve the design and quality of most stock boats. One problem is that while the safety standards are intended to be minimum standards, many manufacturers seem to use them as the basis for building their boats. In other words, they use them as one might wish they would use Lloyd's standards, which many people consider the best available general guide to scantlings and construction methods. Some design and construction techniques commonly used on stock boats could not possibly pass any rational test. Do not assume that the existence of the Boating Safety Act means that a manufacturer will automatically deliver a safe boat.

The boat owner is responsible for meeting certain safety requirements, such as having the required fire extinguishers and life jackets aboard and ensuring proper ventilation of the engine compartment. There are also lighting requirements. Pamphlets detailing the requirements, which vary with the type and size of the vessel, are available from the Coast Guard.

Considerable confusion exists as to the applicability of certain requirements to floating houses without engines. Check on these in the area where the floating house will be moored.

Of vital concern are bans against living aboard boats. At the present time, there are no federal or state laws on this subject. In Hawaii a bill has been introduced to make it illegal to use a boat as a residence in any of the state's harbors. Opponents of boat residents usually have three main complaints: (1) the residents pay cheap rent, (2) they don't pay their fair share of taxes, and (3) they pollute.

As long as anyone who wishes to live in a boat is free to do so, cheap rent seems fair, since anyone who complains about paying more for land living has the option of taking up the boat life. There may be some validity in Hawaii to the complaint about taxes, but many states have remedied the inequity by simply changing the law. Before Hawaii could do this, however, it would have to recognize boats as a legitimate form of housing, something the state seems reluctant to do. It should be noted that there is only limited marina space, and many people feel that it should be used only for recreational boating. As far as the pollution complaint goes, every boat owner is subject to the same pollution laws. No evidence has been presented to show that boat dwellers do any more or any less polluting than any other boat owners. It seems to me that the real problem behind the complaints may be envy of the way boat dwellers seem to enjoy life.

Most public marinas in states other than Hawaii are controlled by city or county regulations. Find out if there are any regulations against boat living in the area where you intend to live.

Taxes

Taxes vary from state to state. The main ones of concern to boat dwellers are the sales tax (generally paid at the time of purchase or registration of boat) and property and/or use tax. Before buying a boat to live in, find out if these taxes are applicable in your area, and if so, how much they will be. In some states (for example, California), a homeowner's property tax exemption of $1,750 on the assessed value of the property applies to a boat that is used as a permanent residence. However, they don't go out of their way to let people know this, and one has to file a form by a certain date each year in order to be eligible.

Insurance

While people have different opinions about the need for insurance coverage on their boats, I think most would agree that it is worth the cost. Among the many types of boat insurance policies, the all-risk

or comprehensive policy, which insures against most things that
could conceivably happen, is recommended. Typical policies are on
a $50 or $100 deductible basis. Such items as outboard motors and
boating gear can usually be included in the same policy. The coverage should include personal liability (if it is not covered by another
policy), property damage, and bodily injury.

Make certain that the insurance policy applies to boats that are being occupied full time. Most policies do. This seems logical, since
most claims are a result of damages occurring either when boats are
in operation or when they are docked or anchored with no one
aboard.

Since boat insurance is an extremely variable item, it pays to shop
around. But remember, the cheapest insurance is not always the best
buy. Some boat insurers have a reputation for doing everything possible to avoid or delay paying claims. Generally, a company specializing in marine insurance is the best bet. Make sure that the policy is
worded to give coverage in the areas and for the time period when
the boat will be in the water, which is usually year round.

As a rough guide to help in planning, one insurance company
quoted the following rates for hull insurance and liability coverage
in a single policy in California at the time of this writing: $100
annually for a $5,000 boat; $175 for a $10,000 boat; $250 for a
$15,000 boat; and $300 for a $20,000 boat.

6 BUYING A BOAT

The purchase of a boat home is a large matter, both in terms of money and the bearing it can have on your life. Thus, it should be given due consideration. The three primary ways of buying discussed here are: (1) buying a new factory-built boat, (2) buying a new custom-built boat, and (3) buying a used boat. Another means of acquiring a boat — building her all or in part — is covered in Chapter 7.

Becoming an informed buyer

Educating yourself is an important step on the path to selecting and buying a boat, and one that is often not given the time it deserves. Unless you are a highly informed buyer, you will be at the mercy of others. You can get advice from other people, for instance by hiring a marine surveyor to act in your interests, but this is no substitute for being knowledgeable yourself. Besides, professional advice is usually sought at an advanced stage, after you have made a tentative selection. And beware of all advice from anyone selling boats. These people are likely to be interested primarily in making money. Fitting you with the right boat is a secondary consideration, if it enters the picture at all.

Stock boats

Regardless of whether you intend eventually to buy a new or used boat, or intend to have one custom built or to build your own, you should begin by studying stock boats for several months. All too often, people buy before they even know what is available. Regardless of the temptation, do not rush into buying any boat.

New boats can be seen at boat shows and boat dealers. Boat shows offer the opportunity to compare many different types and brands of boats, while expending a minimum of time and effort. Dealers' showrooms, on the other hand, allow you more time to study the boats and get answers to your questions.

I suggest that you visit all of the dealers who carry anything even remotely similar to what you have in mind. Even though I'm primarily interested in sailboats, I've found it helpful to study every possible type of vessel. Many ideas from powerboats have been applicable to my sailboat.

When looking, ask questions and have the salesman show you the boats. Pick up the brochures, and ask to see all of the special features listed. Ask about prices: what is included in the base price, what is the cost of optional extras, what are all other charges, such as launching and commissioning? Refrain from expounding your own knowledge of boats. Remember, at this point you are studying, not shopping. A salesman may ask salesman-school questions, such as, "How much can you afford to spend?" Put up with it at this point, but remember that questions like this are ample reason to be skeptical of his advice later when you are ready to buy.

It has been said that only reputable boat dealers can stay in business. I have seen too much evidence to the contrary to put any faith in this. Find out as much about the dealer as possible before buying a boat from him. Check with the local Better Business Bureau. If the dealer has had a number of serious complaints against him, you will probably want to go elsewhere, if there are other dealers in the area that handle the same boat.

Talk to people who have purchased boats from the dealer in question. Find out how long he has been in business. Check whether he has the equipment and professional help to make repairs to meet his guarantees. If he doesn't, find out how he takes care of this. If you have done your homework, you should be able to tell whether the dealer knows boats. This is important; while many dealers are in boating themselves, others use it merely as a way to make a living. I know of one dealer, for example, who hates boating, doesn't go out himself, and doesn't even like to go out on demonstrations with customers.

As far as stock boats are concerned, buying a new boat will probably allow you to come closest to exactly what you want, but generally it will cost more than a similarly equipped used boat of the same model. Also, keep in mind that, with the increase in cost of both raw materials and labor, many manufacturers have lowered the quality of models that have been in production over a period of years.

Custom-built boats

Custom-built boats almost always cost more than similar factory-production models. The basic premise is that the boat will be closer to the owner's exact requirements. However, whenever money is an important consideration, custom-built boats are a risky way to go about getting what you want. I've heard of many bad experiences. In some cases, the final bill has been double the original estimate.

The above caution applies mainly to functional boats. For floating houses, the situation is quite different. After the raft part of a floating home is built, the remainder of the construction is more like a land house than a boat. Thus, custom-built models become quite practical, and most new models are constructed and sold in this manner. Two established firms specializing in floating houses are: Sea View Floating Homes, Inc., 1884 N. W. North River Drive, Miami, Florida 33125; and Lakehurst Floating Homes, 820 Grand, Alameda, California 94501. One-bedroom floating houses start at about $10,000.

Used boats

Unlike automobiles, quality used boats generally have a high resale value. This is especially true of fiberglass boats. A first step is locating boats that are on the market.

Listings. Listings of used boats are found in newspapers and boating magazines. Or visit a boat broker or boat dealer. Typical information in newspapers and boating magazines includes: type and size of boat, main hull construction material (wood, fiberglass, steel, etc.), accommodations ("sleeps four"), main features ("boat has galley, dinette, enclosed head"), and power (type of engine).

There are also a number of boat locating services. Some of these are computerized, but this is largely a gimmick. Be careful, since you will be paying for a service designed to lure you into buying, and often for information that you could find on your own. However, there are times when these services may be desirable, especially if you are looking for a particular boat that is difficult to find. These services are advertised in boating magazines and newspapers, and they are listed in telephone directories.

Marinas and boatyards. Marinas and boatyards, plus waterfront areas in boating regions, are good places to look for used boats.

Boat dealers. Boat dealers sometimes are a source of used boats. Some of them take used boats in trade, although this is much less frequent than is the case with automobiles, especially in the larger sizes of boats. Often the dealer is merely acting as a broker, perhaps on an arrangement providing that if he sells the used boat, then the other person will buy a new one from him. In most cases, you can expect to pay a top price for a used boat from a dealer.

Brokers. It is common practice to buy and sell more costly boats through brokers. Brokers typically work on a commission basis, demanding generally 10 percent of the selling price up to a certain amount, usually about $50,000, then seven percent thereafter. This means that the buyer ends up paying a correspondingly higher price than if he purchased the boat directly from the seller. Why, then, does anyone use a broker's services? For someone selling a boat, a broker can give the demonstration trials and handle paper work and the transfer of large sums of money. Loan institutions seem to prefer to work through a broker, making financing somewhat easier for the buyer to obtain if he buys from a broker.

But the buyer is paying indirectly for the services of the broker, so it is important to select a broker carefully. Make certain that the broker is licensed and bonded, if that is required in your state. Thoroughly check the reputation of the broker.

An advantage of buying through a broker frequently mentioned in the brokers' advertising sections of boating magazines is that the broker is an expert and can fit the right boat to the right owner. This is generally nonsense. While I realize that there are brokers with good reputations who are both competent and ethical, I know of many brokers who do not fit that description. I've known, for example, a number of people shopping for sailboats for world cruising who found that, almost without exception, the brokers they approached tried to sell them whatever they happened to have as being suitable.

I've seen so many brokers using the tricks of an unscrupulous used-car salesman that I have become highly skeptical of brokers in general. To most of them a customer is apparently little more than a pawn in a game. At any rate, expect to be pressured into buying, and be on the lookout for "selling psychology," such as:

(1) "If you don't hurry and buy this one, you will miss out and you'll never have an opportunity like this again." Forget this "opportunity," and avoid making a rush decision.

(2) Suggestions that the boat you want is not good enough for you, followed by a sales pitch for one that costs more.

The steps in buying a boat from a broker, which vary in different parts of the United States, might go something like this:

(1) The broker will show you and allow you to board any boats he has listed that you think you might be interested in. There are two main types of listings: *closed*, which are handled exclusively by one broker; and *open*, which are also listed by other brokers.

(2) If you find a boat that you are interested in buying, you can pay a deposit (generally 10 percent of the selling price of the boat), which is refundable under a number of stated conditions. In most cases the money will be refunded if you do not buy the boat. Make sure, however, that you know exactly what the conditions for the refund are, and that these conditions will allow you to recover your deposit should you decide not to buy the boat. Important conditions that should be clearly spelled out are that you be able to obtain financing and that the demonstration be to your satisfaction. The final purchase should also depend on a satisfactory survey. Finally, make sure that you also can turn down the boat strictly on your own opinion. You can also make any other stipulations you desire at this time, for instance, that certain repairs be made on the boat, which the owner can accept or reject. If the owner rejects your requests, then the deposit should be refundable.

In almost every case, it is a good idea to make a lower offer, as it is common practice to ask more for a boat than the minimum that would be accepted. Of course, the seller has the option of rejecting any offer lower than the asking price. If the first offer is rejected, the buyer can make a higher offer, or the owner may make a counter-offer, which can be rejected or accepted by the prospective buyer. In most cases the potential buyer must make the deposit before any offers are presented to the seller.

(3) After the deposit is made and an offer accepted, the next step is to obtain financing. Don't allow the broker to make any stipulations in the initial agreement regarding financing. Should you change your mind, you will want to be able to say simply that you could not obtain "satisfactory" financing. Do not make an agreement that depends on your obtaining a loan from a certain bank or other loan institution, especially one recommended by the broker. Be especially leery of brokers who have the loan application papers ready for you to fill out. Sometimes, and I feel that this is preferable for the buyer, a demonstration of the boat is allowed first.

(4) A demonstration is given. If you don't know much about boats, take along someone to advise you, even if you have to pay for

his services. After the demonstration, the salesman will probably try to get you to sign a statement that the boat is acceptable. Don't do it. Take all the time allowed in the contract (the deposit basically is an agreement to hold the boat for your consideration until a certain specified date) before making a final decision. If you sign, the easiest way of getting out of buying later is eliminated. Maintain the option of saying that the boat is unsatisfactory as long as possible.

If the demonstration is given before you obtain financing, then you still have this way out. Of course, if financing was required before the demonstration (and pending satisfactory survey), then you have already eliminated your option to terminate the purchase on financial grounds, should you change your mind.

(5) The next step is a survey, which usually requires a haul-out. The prospective buyer generally is required to pay for both the haul-out and the survey, and the survey can be made by anyone he wants, provided the survey is acceptable to the loan institution, if any, that is financing the boat. If the buyer is paying cash, then the survey is strictly optional. However, unless the buyer is an expert on boats, a survey is recommended (see section below on "Surveys").

If the boat does not pass the survey, the boat can be rejected, and all of the deposit money (after the haul-out and surveyor's fees have been paid) is refunded. Other possibilities include requiring that the owner make the necessary corrections so that the boat will be able to pass the survey, or the buyer can make the repairs at his expense if that is required to obtain a loan, or the buyer can accept the boat just as it is.

(6) After a satisfactory survey, or the buyer's waiver of the survey, the final step is the completion of the financial transactions and signing over of the title to the new owner. The original deposit, of course, is applied to the purchase cost. It should be noted and considered ahead of time that there probably will be other costs, such as state sales tax, insurance (optional if boat isn't financed, but desirable anyway), and property tax (which usually becomes the buyer's responsibility starting on the date of purchase, to be paid after the tax year). In some cases, however, the buyer will be held responsible for any unpaid taxes for the taxable year, so make sure that these have been taken care of. If there's a property or use tax on boats in your state, check thoroughly on all rules and regulations. The broker should have this information.

Evaluating a boat

Whether new or used, a boat should be evaluated carefully before purchase. In the case of a custom-built floating home or boat, make certain that everything is satisfactory before final acceptance.

Inspection. The prospective buyer should know enough about boats to make his own inspection, in addition to getting whatever outside advice he can. Make sure that the boat is suitable for whatever you intend to do with it. Carefully examine the construction and condition. This applies equally to new boats, as shoddy and inadequate construction, in spite of federal safety standards, is commonplace. (References for information about construction methods and materials are given in the Appendix.)

Sea trial. Give the boat a sea trial. When buying a new boat, even if a sea trial has been given in a "demonstrator," take a trial run in the boat you will actually purchase before finally accepting her. A sea trial should be at least four to six hours long. Also, if sea or weather conditions are unsuitable (for instance, no wind or too much wind when trying out a sailboat), insist on a second sea trial on a better day.

Sometimes a buyer considers the sea trial a lesson in operating the boat, but this purpose should be strictly secondary to determining whether the boat performs satisfactorily.

Survey. A survey is not a guarantee. Regardless of what the surveyor concludes, you will have little or no legal recourse if his opinions prove to be false. A survey is an opinion (hopefully a professional one), and nothing more. If the surveyor is competent and honest, then his opinion can be extremely valuable. However, licensing requirements are minimal or nonexistent in most states, which means that almost anyone can legally hang out a shingle declaring that he is a marine surveyor. Thus, it is extremely important to select a surveyor carefully. Talk to people who have had surveys made. Check with the Better Business Bureau. If there have been complaints against the surveyor, reject him, and even if no complaints have been made, remember that this does not guarantee competence and honesty.

I have noticed that surveyors in general seem reluctant to find things wrong with boats, and they are inclined to overlook certain defects. Perhaps they are afraid of losing future business, and want to avoid antagonizing dealers and brokers by finding things wrong with boats that scare off potential buyers. Even though the buyer pays for the survey, and in some states it is considered unethical and even illegal for dealers and brokers to recommend surveyors, surveyors tend to slant their opinions to the advantage of the dealers and brokers.

Nevertheless, a survey generally is worth the money, whether or not it is required for obtaining a loan. The surveyor may be able to find weaknesses and defects of which the buyer is unaware, even though the buyer has done his homework.

A new boat should be surveyed, too. Don't take anything for granted just because the boat is new. The worst boats can be eliminated quickly by anyone who has studied construction methods.

Make sure you know what is included in the survey. Will the machinery be surveyed? The performance? You will be given a written report describing the condition, defects, and value of the boat. It is also important to be there when the survey is made, as the surveyor can often point out things that you need to consider.

Standard equipment and optional extras

A "base" price is given for most new boats, but in most cases the buyer will need much additional equipment; in some cases the "base" price will be doubled before the transaction is completed. This explains why some used boats can be sold for more than the base price of a new boat of the same model. The difference is in the extras, and these are often of considerable value. Since few stock boats are designed specifically for boat living, some additional equipment and modifications are almost always needed (see Chapters 4 and 8). When comparing prices, keep in mind extra equipment. When buying either a new or a used boat, you can probably save money by doing some of the modifications and equipping yourself.

Financing

Financing a boat is relatively simple, often too simple, for it is here that many people get stuck with more than they bargain for. Those convenient monthly payments don't seem so convenient when they come due with mechanical regularity. I may be old-fashioned, but I believe that the installment plan is one of the least desirable avenues to a boat.

If $10,000 of the cost of a boat is financed over a seven-year period at 10 percent annual simple interest, the interest rate for each year is $1,000, so for the seven years the total interest will be $7,000, or 70 percent of the original amount borrowed. And at the time of writing, it is difficult to obtain an interest rate this low. On 10-year loans, the interest is likely to be more than the amount borrowed in the first place.

Perhaps paying large sums in interest can be justified if the payments are made with money that would have been used for some other type of housing, but I suggest that the buyer examine other possibilities, not involving a large loan, before taking the financial plunge. Consider, for example, that building a fiberglass kit boat (see Chapter 7) might keep you out of debt, because you can partially complete the boat, launch her, move in, and then finish her gradually over a period of time as the money becomes available.

Until quite recently, it was difficult to finance a boat, but many banks and loan institutions now welcome such business and will finance both new and used boats. At least 10 percent down is usually required on a new boat, and 20 percent or more on a used one. It is difficult to get a loan on "home-made" and unconventional boats. The loan institution will be looking at the condition and value of the boat and the financial situation of the potential buyer.

Most loan institutions will require a survey on any used boat; in some cases a survey will be required on a new boat. "Actual value" usually is determined with a price book (similar to the *Blue Book* used for automobiles) and the surveyor's report. The lender will examine the potential buyer's credit record and his general financial picture to make sure that he will be able to meet the expenses involved in addition to making the loan payments.

Shop around for the most favorable loan, since interest rates vary. Some institutions charge an interest penalty in the event of early payoff.

Trade-ins

Only a few boat dealers, and even fewer brokers, will accept boats in trade. Trading a boat — or for that matter a house, automobile, mobile home, camper, or anything else — is sometimes advantageous on a private basis (no broker involved). It all depends on whether or not you can find someone who wants what you have, and has what you want. Either way, buying privately or through a broker or dealer, you will be in the best bargaining position when you have cash. This means that it is generally advantageous to sell an old boat rather than to plan on trading her. When selling, allow as much time as possible. A rush sale almost always brings in less money.

If you do want to look for a trade, a classified ad is worth a try. Make sure that you know what you want.

Warranties and guarantees

Get all warranties and guarantees in writing. Make certain they clearly spell out how and by whom the repairs and adjustments are to be made, should they become necessary. I know of a number of boat owners who have had difficulties getting manufacturers to honor their guarantees, or found themselves responsible for expensive shipping charges on boat equipment sent to the factory for repairs. Fine print in the warranties and guarantees can considerably reduce their value. All too often, the only way to get a manufacturer to honor a guarantee is to file suit against him, something that many boat owners cannot afford to do, as the manufacturers are well aware.

On the more positive side, there are many companies that will go out of their way to make good on their guarantees. But determining which companies are which can be difficult, and is often left to chance.

Commissioning

Commissioning applies primarily to new boats. It is basically the dealer's preparation of the boat, and it may or may not include launching. Commissioning is often an optional extra, and sometimes the cost is considerable. Be sure you understand what this will cost and what is included. If you have the necessary skills, you may want to do your own commissioning. Often this requires no more skill than is necessary to maintain the boat properly.

Many dealers will include the repair of factory defects, such as cracks and chips in gel coats on fiberglass boats, in the commissioning. This should be done without cost to the buyer.

Boat slip

Sometimes, when buying a boat for a home, you can make it a condition of the sale that the dealer or broker obtain a slip for you. This is especially desirable in areas where slips are hard to find.

7 BUILDING A BOAT

Building the boat yourself is another way of achieving your goal. You will save money and have the satisfaction of doing your own work. While there have certainly been many failures, which amount to broken and abandoned dreams, there have also been many home-built successes, some remarkable ones.

Boatbuilding from plans

Building a boat from the ground up is a large project, to say the least, and one that should not be undertaken lightly. For the right person it can be meaningful and worthwhile; for the wrong person, it can end as a disaster.

The amateur builder is wise to start with plans for a proven design, plans drawn up with the amateur builder in mind.

I know of several boats that were designed by the builders themselves, but none of these people could really be considered "amateur." Almost all had had considerable experience designing and building boats, whether through vocation or as a sideline to their regular means of making a living.

Amateur boatbuilding failures result from lack of skill and gross underestimations of the cost and time required. While demands made on the builder vary greatly with design, size, and construction methods and materials, building any boat from the ground up is hard, slow work. New materials and building techniques are purported to make boatbuilding easier and less time-consuming, and this is true, but only relatively so. In most cases, building a boat takes thousands of hours of labor, and if it's a spare-time project it can take many years.

The temptation to give up on a large boatbuilding project is related directly to the time it requires. Greatly underestimating at the start the time required, many builders give up at some point along the way, discouraged because the completed boat is still nowhere in sight.

Success depends on realistic appraisal of your existing and potential boatbuilding skill and innovativeness, and careful estimation of money and time needed for completion of the project.

Below are some of the main types of amateur boat construction:

(1) Traditional wood construction, generally planked. A good-quality job takes considerable skill and patience, and anything less is essentially worthless. Plans for a number of proven designs are readily available, many at low cost. For example, plans for the well-proven and long-popular Tahiti ketch are available from Fawcett Plans Service, Fawcett Building, Greenwich, Connecticut 06830 (Plan No. B-104), for just eight dollars.

I feel that one of the advantages of this type of construction is that wood is satisfying to work with. A disadvantage is the high cost of wood and the difficulty in finding high-quality lumber.

(2) Cold-molded wood construction. This method, in which thin sheets of wood are glued together over a mold to form the desired hull shape, has proven quite successful for amateur construction. While a number of skilled operations are required, once these are mastered it is mainly a matter of doing the same thing over and over again. Compound curves are possible. The final result is essentially a one-piece hull made of plywood. Frequently the hull is sheathed in fiberglass.

Plans are easily available for a number of types and designs of boats suitable for cold-molded construction. This method is frequently used for multihull boats, especially where a high strength-per-weight ratio is required.

(3) Plywood. A number of boats have been especially designed for plywood construction. Since compound curves are not possible from a single sheet of plywood, most of the boats are hard-chine designs. This is perhaps the most practical construction method for amateurs building from the ground up. Plywood boats can be sheathed in fiberglass for added protection.

Almost all types of boats — floating houses, houseboats, power cruisers, and sailboats; monohulls, catamarans, and trimarans — have been built successfully from plywood by amateurs. One big disadvantage of this material is its high cost.

(4) Ferrocement. Ferrocement has been promoted as the material that will enable any amateur to build a boat quickly at low cost. In practice, a few first-class boats have been made by amateurs from this material (and more recent variations), many shoddy boats have been built, and perhaps an even larger number of failures have been abandoned.

There are many problems associated with the use of ferrocement. While plastering the hull may not take long, it takes most people months to construct the frames and lay up the wire mesh, then many hours more after the plastering to achieve a smooth professional finish, something that few amateurs manage. And although the hull may be the most important and difficult part, it generally represents considerably less than half the finished boat in terms of both time and money. Ferrocement has been promoted as being much less expensive than other materials, but even if this is true, finishing out a boat in a high-quality manner involves the same difficulty and costs, whether she has a ferrocement hull or a hull of another material. The low cost of a ferrocement hull has tempted many amateur builders to start on boats that are much larger than they would otherwise attempt. The result is revealed by numerous advertisements like the following: "50 ft. ferrocement sailboat, partially completed. Make offer. Will consider any trade."

Ferrocement boats frequently are built by amateurs in rental yards devoted to this material and type of construction. Supposedly professional guidance is available, but several visits recently to large yards of this type were unconvincing to me. Before you launch into a ferrocement boat project, I suggest that you carefully consider your boat as she will look when finished, how long she will take to complete, how much work will be involved, and how much she will cost. While there are many useful and valuable books on ferrocement boatbuilding, I highly recommend Bruce Bingham's *Ferro-cement: Design, Techniques and Application* (Cambridge, Maryland: Cornell Maritime Press, Inc., 1974).

(5) Fiberglass. A basic problem with fiberglass boat construction for amateur builders is the high cost of constructing female molds. Manufacturers absorb this cost by making many boats from the same mold. For one-off boat construction, techniques have been developed to get around this problem. A male mold of one sort or another is used, and it is often shaped from a foam-core material laid up over

temporary frames and longitudinals. The hull is generally started upside-down. After the exterior is fiberglassed, the hull is turned upright, the frames are removed, and the interior is fiberglassed. One problem with this technique is that it is extremely difficult to achieve a smooth, fair finish, although it can be done. Several professional boatbuilding firms are using this method for one-off boatbuilding. However, unless the amateur builder has a special reason for wanting to construct the hull, for instance, to build an original design, I would strongly suggest that he purchase a professionally molded hull from a stock-boat manufacturer. Many are available (see section below on building from hulls and kits).

(6) Steel. A few amateurs have built boats from steel, and this method may be more practical than it first appears. While a certain amount of special equipment is involved, and special skills need to be mastered, the equipment is often no more expensive, nor the skills more difficult, than those needed for building boats from other materials. Many community colleges and adult education programs offer classes and courses in metal work and welding, with low or nonexistent tuition fees.

For all of the above construction methods, it is possible to buy someone out and then take over the construction. Many partially completed, amateur-built boats are offered for sale. There are many reasons why the original builders give up or are forced to sell: one has money problems, another discovers that he doesn't have enough skill and the boat is turning out a mess, still another has a change in his original reasons or goals for building the boat.

Often these unfinished boats are hopeless and not worth considering, but not always. The original builder may have been doing a skilled, first-class construction job, and the boat may be offered for sale for some reason other than poor construction. It takes a person with considerable knowledge and experience with boats to determine this, however. For the less knowledgeable, this way of acquiring a boat is not recommended. Most amateur-built boats have little resale value, so these partly built boats are inexpensive, but make certain you aren't merely making someone else's bad dream your own.

For some people, building a boat from plans — from the ground up — is the most meaningful way to acquire a boat home. It takes true dedication to the do-it-yourself idea, however, and for people who don't feel strongly dedicated, it is better to start with a professionally built hull or floats.

Boatbuilding from hulls and kits

Fifteen years ago, kits for wooden boats were readily available. Only a few now remain on the market. These come in a number of variations, including frame kits, kits with everything except plywood, and complete kits. The component parts are typically preshaped, and even a frame kit, which saves the builder from doing the lofting, can be a big advantage over building from plans.

Several companies offer float or raft components for constructing floating homes and houseboats. These are available in a number of materials, of which the most common are fiberglass and other plastics, aluminum, and steel. They are often foam filled. An important advantage of starting with these professionally built components is that you have a good "foundation." Also, most components are sold with detailed plans and instructions for assembling them. Since the house or cabin structures that are added can often be box-shaped, the construction can be quite simple compared with most types of boatbuilding.

Another possibility — and I feel that this is a good one — is to buy a pontoon or raft kit with decking and then add a trailer house for the living accommodations. Good used trailer houses are often available for $1,000 to $3,000. Several companies make floating components especially for this purpose; others can be adapted. I know of one couple who used a $2,000 raft kit and a $1,500 trailer house to create their home. With a stern-mounted outboard motor, she is a functional boat.

In some examples of this combination, the trailer house can be taken off and still used on land; in others, the trailer house has the wheels removed and is mounted permanently on the float.

Fiberglass hulls, with or without component kits for completing the boat, offer the amateur builder a means of getting a good boat and saving money in the process. In *Fiberglass Kit Boats* (Camden, Maine: International Marine Publishing Company, 1973), I covered this exciting approach to a boat, detailed the construction methods and skills required, and compiled a list of manufacturers of hulls and kits. In the course of researching the book, I had the opportunity of seeing the results of hundreds of amateurs' efforts. Contrary to what I have seen in ferrocement construction, I saw almost no shattered dreams with the fiberglass kit boats. Even in the few cases where for one reason or another the original builder sold out before completing

Figure 20. *The Dreadnought 32, a popular live-aboard and world-cruising sailboat, is available in kit form from Dreadnought Boatworks, Carpinteria, California. (Photo by author.)*

the project, seldom did he lose much money, and in a couple of instances he actually made money on the deal.

Even starting with the minimum bare hull, supplying your own materials, and constructing the remainder of the boat yourself, you are way ahead of the "ground-up" boatbuilder. However, you still have to avoid one of the greatest pitfalls of building fiberglass kit boats, which is the tendency to construct unsightly cabins and deck-houses. It is here that many amateur builders deviate from the designer's plans. Keep in mind that construction of a deck and cabin top is a major boatbuilding task.

Most home builders start with at least the hull, deck and cabin structure, and rudder. Most manufacturers will supply some or all of the components and materials for finishing the boats. Often these are divided into a series of component kits, which make the buy-when-you-can-afford-it plan practical, resulting in savings from not having to pay interest on a boat loan.

Several manufacturers will also sell their boats at "any stage of completion," so the more difficult jobs, such as installing engines and ballast, can be done at the factory.

Because leading boat manufacturers are now offering the same designs in kit form as they sell as completed boats, the builder has a large selection of types, designs, and sizes to choose from. Even some famous offshore cruising sailboats that were originally wood designs are now offered in fiberglass as bare hulls with or without component kits.

An important consideration is the possibility of living in kit boats when they are only partially completed. A number of people have done this, living aboard in the water or in a do-it-yourself boatyard and gradually completing the boat as the money becomes available, sometimes over a period of years. Completing the interior in this manner may mean living with paint cans and tools and half-finished furnishings, but many feel that it is worth it, and many could not otherwise afford a boat home. Money is saved because you provide labor; materials and supplies can be purchased at discount prices; and interest on a large boat loan is avoided.

You might also consider the possibility of buying a fiberglass kit boat that someone else has started. These are sometimes available, and you may be able to find just what you want for less than the manufacturer's price. However, check carefully on the quality of the work that has been done on the boat.

Conversions

There are many conversion possibilities. For example, lifeboats, whaleboats, and workboats have all been converted into residences. For anyone considering this, excellent books on the subject are: *Small Craft Conversion* by John Lewis (London: Adlard Coles, 1972) and *Boat Repairs and Conversions* by Michael Verney (Camden, Maine: International Marine Publishing Company, 1972). These books not only cover the hows and whys, but also give specific examples. Keep in mind, however, that adding cabins and accommodations may be the easy part of the conversion; making a boat functional can be a more difficult matter. Converting powerboats to sailboats can be especially difficult.

Damaged and neglected boats

Boatyards around the country are filled with an assortment of damaged boats. Before buying one, make a realistic evaluation of the extent of damage and the amount of time, skill, and money that will be required for repair.

Wooden boats with dry rot or worms are generally the cheapest and most readily available. However, unless you know what you're doing, I would suggest that you forget about these.

Damaged fiberglass boats are generally a much better possibility, as the fiberglass is at least free of dry rot and worms. Even extensively damaged boats have been restored by amateurs, but it often takes a fairly innovative person to do this.

Neglected boats are sometimes a good buy, especially if only cleaning and cosmetic work are needed. Again, check wooden boats carefully for dry rot and worms, as this is often the reason why someone gave up on them in the first place.

Other considerations

For all types of boatbuilding, be sure to take into account the cost of space rental, sales tax, transportation and shipping charges, equipment rentals, and professional help.

8 MODIFYING AND EQUIPPING A BOAT

Since everyone seems to have his or her own idea of what a boat home should be, few stock boats are exactly right. While building a complete boat requires special skills and dedication, modifying and equipping tasks fall within the capabilities of many with less skill and time.

In *Modifying Fiberglass Boats* (Camden, Maine: International Marine Publishing Company, 1975), I detailed hundreds of modifications. Other sources of information are included in the Appendix of this book.

If you do the work yourself, you save money, you enjoy the satisfaction of doing it, and you can do the job the way you want it. Installation of many manufactured products is quite easy, often requiring no more skill than will be necessary to maintain them. Most manufactured items come with installation instructions, and these should be followed carefully. Of course, you can have some or all of the work done for you.

Modifying

The primary reason for modifying a boat is to make your home more comfortable and convenient — in other words, more livable. Other reasons for making modifications — to make the boat safer, to improve her performance, to improve her appearance — are generally secondary concerns, but any modifications should not adversely affect these factors.

Successful modifications require careful planning. Make certain you have the necessary equipment and skill before attempting anything on the boat. Do your practicing and learning away from the boat, perhaps with scrap materials. As a general guide, no modification should be made on the boat until you are capable of doing work that is in keeping with the rest of the boat in terms of both quality and appearance.

Modifications that can seriously affect the performance and safety of a vessel, such as increasing the size of the cabin and adding deckhouses and after cabins, can have disastrous results when they are attempted by those who know little about boats and the sea. Major design changes should be made only with the approval of a professional boat designer.

There are many types of modifications, however, that can be made without seriously affecting performance or safety. Typical jobs are: adding shelves and racks, rearranging counter space and storage compartments, installing drawers, improving doors, and modifying berths (removing one or more berths and improving the ones that remain).

Adding to one thing in a boat usually means subtracting from something else. Perhaps the most frequent sacrifice is in the number of berths. In making modifications, be careful not to remove sections

Figure 21. *A battery charger is mounted in a drop-in panel. (Photo by author.)*

A. Medicine cabinet
B Handrails
C Pin rails
D Dish, cup & towel rack
E Laminated tillers

Figure 22. Left: *Teak and mahogany marine accessories can be installed quickly either by factory workmen or by do-it-yourselfers.* Right: *A compact yet adequate galley rack. (Courtesy H & L Marine Woodwork, Inc.)*

that are designed to strengthen and stiffen the hull. When in doubt, check first with the designer or manufacturer of the boat.

A few subassemblies, such as fiberglass galleys with recessed sink and stove, shower stalls, and a wide variety of cabinets and racks, are now being manufactured. While buying these components is more expensive than constructing your own, they can make things easier, as you have only the installation to do, which is often quite easy.

Replacing nonopening ports with opening ones also involves buying equipment (see next section). A number of modifications can be made to improve ventilation, such as adding cabin vents. Most often, factory components are used, and these come with instructions and fasteners for installing them. Dorade vents seem best for sea. Cutouts and louvers might be added to compartment and storage-compartment doors for improved air circulation.

In some areas screening will be a must, and stock boats seldom have any. Snap-in screens are available for many manufactured opening ports and windows. Some vents, such as the Tannoy, come with a built-in screen, but others do not. Adding a screen generally is a simple modification.

Screening hatches and companionways can be accomplished by using a Touch'n'Hold screening system. Kits are available from Velcro Marine Products, 681 Fifth Avenue, New York, New York 10022. Again, installation is simple.

People who live aboard stock boats often complain about the galley sink, which in the typical new boat is a tiny one made of molded fiberglass. Many people replace it with a larger one of stainless steel.

A good way to add a shower is to purchase a shower stall and sump specially designed for boats. Provided there's enough space, installation should not be too difficult, although plumbing, of course, will be required. Keep in mind that a major complaint against showers is that they add moisture to the interior of the boat. The shower stall should be a chamber sealed off from the rest of the boat's interior, and the shower compartment should be vented directly outside. It usually takes two vents, one drawing air in, the other taking it out, to provide effective ventilation. Another common problem with showers is dry rot in wood in areas surrounding the shower stall, for instance, in a wooden bulkhead that connects with a plastic or fiberglass stall. For this reason, fiberglass shower stalls are often bonded directly to the fiberglass hull with no intervening wooden parts.

If you have a shore connection for water, a bathtub can be an

Figure 23. *The Tannoy air vent is a frequent modification added by boat dwellers. (Photo by author.)*

asset. A number of small plastic models, many of which take up only slightly more space than a shower stall, are available from camper and travel-trailer supply stores. In many cases a bathtub/ shower combination presents no greater installation problem than a shower alone.

A number of laws have been enacted in parts of the United States to control or ban the discharge of sewage into the water. State laws vary, and there are no national laws. Also, there is a gap between laws and enforcement. To add to the confusion, a number of firms have made a racket of selling overpriced, and often poorly designed and built, equipment, sometimes falsely claiming that it is needed to satisfy the law. As a result, some boat owners have installed holding tanks in areas where there are no pump-out facilities, and there has arisen a continuous need for expensive chemicals of questionable value. A tank that allows 40 uses between trips to a pump-out station probably won't be very convenient: a 20-gallon holding tank is about minimum for daily use. The time between pump-outs can be extended by means of a recirculating system, but caution is advised here, as many of the systems on the market are far from odorless, most often because of sealing valves that fail to seal completely. Boat-show demonstrations mean little. Try to find out from other boat dwellers what, if anything, works in practice. In my trimaran I had an early model of a recirculating toilet, which was unsatisfactory because the odor of the chemicals themselves was offensive. I have heard a positive report from a family I know on their Monogram recirculating unit (nonelectric), which is charged with fresh water and chemicals. Developing an effective toilet system seems to involve real problems of design, engineering, and construction. Hopefully, the present systems will be improved in the not-too-distant future. Holding tanks come in various sizes, types, and designs, and installation of most of them should be within the capabilities of most boat owners.

Equipping

Even if you buy a new boat, you can save money by buying her without some of the equipment and then purchasing the equipment at discount prices and installing it yourself.

A number of possibilities for equipping a boat are given in Chapter 4. This chapter is mainly concerned with the purchase of equipment you can install yourself.

Figure 24. *The Monomatic electrical recirculating marine toilet requires a precharge of only 4 gallons of water. (Courtesy Monogram Industries, Inc.)*

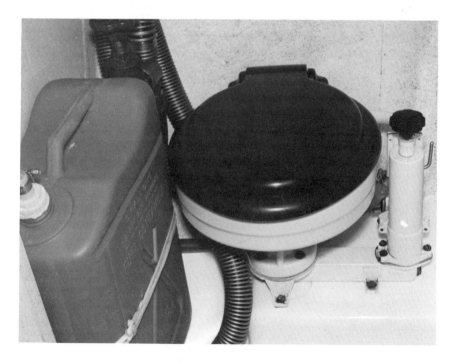

Figure 25. *A fuel container is converted to serve as a holding tank where space is at a premium. (Photo by author.)*

A key step to saving money on marine equipment is price shopping. While equipment intended for land houses and trailer houses and motor homes is frequently suitable for floating houses, and sometimes for houseboats, marine quality is recommended for all other types. But even with this in mind, price shopping can result in considerable savings. There are, for example, a number of mail-order firms in the United States that sell brand-name marine equipment and gear at discount prices (see Appendix). Even when postage is added, the cost can be much less than in most marine stores. English equipment can often be purchased at discount prices by ordering directly from England. The savings are often substantial, even after duty and shipping are figured in. A list of English firms that offer mail-order service to American customers is included in the Appendix.

Mail-order catalogs and buyers' guides are handy reference sources. Another possibility is to write directly to the manufacturer for brochures, but I recommend this only if you cannot get the information elsewhere. Mail inquiries are costly to businesses, and lead eventually to a higher cost of the product. Many small businesses cannot afford to answer these types of inquiries. A stamped, self-addressed envelope will improve your chances of getting the information.

9 WHERE TO LIVE

As the number of boats on the waters in the United States has increased, more and more restrictions have been placed on boat living. Restrictions are especially severe in areas where there are few or no natural harbors and artificial harbors have been constructed. Federal waters, which should be for everyone to use, have been taken over by developers and city officials, who in turn not only reap the profits, but also make the rules and regulations, many of which ban boat living.

In any case, the possibility of finding moorage space is an important consideration for anyone contemplating life aboard a boat.

Marinas

Modern marinas have attracted many to the live-aboard life. Probably most of the boat dwellers in the United States moor their boats in marinas, either in slips or at side-ties.

Some marinas are very basic, others are quite elaborate. The better ones have shore facilities akin to country clubs, including amenities such as lounges, recreation rooms, swimming pools, saunas, gymnasiums, restaurants, coffee shops, and so on. The cost of the "extras," of course, is reflected in the cost of the slip rental.

Marinas vary greatly in price and quality, not only from one area of the United States to another, but also within the same geographical area. Prices depend not only on quality, but also on supply and demand. Areas where there are large natural protected waterways, for instance, the East and Gulf coasts, tend to have lower marina fees than areas where many of the harbors are artificial, for instance, certain parts of the West Coast. Also, slip fees are higher in densely populated areas.

Figure 26. Above: *A modern marina.* Below: *A marina in Santa Barbara, California. (Photos by author.)*

While there are still marinas that charge less than fifty cents per boat foot per month, some marinas in areas where the supply of slips is far behind the demand are charging three dollars or more per boat foot a month.

As a general rule, slip rent is based on the length overall, plus bowsprits, boomkins, and other parts of the boat that extend beyond the LOA; or the length of the boat slip, whichever is greater.

There are two types of marina docks: nonfloating (built on pilings) and floating. Nonfloating docks present difficulties in waters where there are large tidal changes, since the height of the dock changes in relation to a moored boat and docking lines and fenders have to be arranged with this in mind. Moderate tide changes can often be accommodated by using special arrangements to take up slack in dock lines, such as pulleys and weights or floating rings or tires that can move up and down over pilings.

Figure 27. *The* Sea Puppy *protected by fenders and moored at a side-tie. (Photo by author.)*

The trend in new marinas is toward floating docks. The floating dock remains the same height in relation to the moored boats, so that problems with fenders and docking lines are minimized.

Boats are moored either by side-ties or in one- and two-boat slips (a slip is formed by two parallel fingers extending from a walkway dock). At many marinas the rent is higher for slips than for side-ties. A single-boat slip is best for live-aboard boats, especially where the water frequently surges around the docks, because the boat can be moored by four lines, which will keep the boat away from the dock. Side-ties and two-boat slips require fenders, and the motion of the boat can be somewhat uncomfortable.

Figure 28. *A length of hose is useful for protecting a dock line from chafing as it runs through the mooring cleat. (Photo by author.)*

I have spent time in all three types of mooring arrangements. In calm waters, all three are satisfactory. In marinas that are not well protected, I think the single-boat slip is worth the extra fee that might be charged.

Some marinas have fenders and rub strakes of rubber or plastic that line all or part of the slip and dock for side-tie arrangements; others have nothing but bare wood or cement or, worse yet, bolts and other protruding objects. In the latter, placement of fenders becomes extremely important if the boat is to be protected from rubbing and scraping against the docks. I think it is a good idea to use fenders even if fenders are attached to the dock, as the ones commonly provided often are inadequate.

Marinas have rules, and where it is a seller's market, the list of rules is likely to be longer. Many of the rules are for the benefit and protection of the slip renters, but all too often rules are added for the convenience of the marina operators.

The most important rule is the one permitting or prohibiting living aboard. If it is permitted, there may be special restrictions that will affect you (such as special fees, rules prohibiting children or pets, etc.).

The legality of prohibiting living in boats is being questioned seriously in many areas. Too often the decision of whether people can live in boats has been left to marina managers, many of whom seem concerned only with making as much money as possible with the least amount of effort. Many people feel that the marinas have been getting away with the restrictions only because they haven't been challenged in the courts. One of the usual reasons given by certain marinas for not allowing living aboard is that boat dwellers use more utilities. But this can be taken care of by charging a special fee or by placing the utilities on separate meters. I have seen both of these methods in use. Typical fees range from about five to twenty dollars extra per month for each person in the boat.

Other rules concern the type of work that can be done on boats and type of rental agreement (month-to-month, lease, amount of deposit, etc.).

The slip-rental cost depends on a number of factors:

(1) Available space
(2) Popularity of the marina
(3) Ownership of the marina (public or private)
(4) Geographic location
(5) Condition and type of facilities available

Many marinas currently have long waiting lists for slips. Although I think it is unfair, many marinas sell boats (a typical sideline of marina operators) by guaranteeing a live-aboard slip with the purchase of a boat.

The most important considerations when selecting a marina are:

(1) How does the marina operate?

(2) Is parking available?

(3) Are there showers, rest rooms, and storage lockers?

(4) What type of security system is used?

Check out the facilities thoroughly. Are electricity and water provided at each slip? Will there be adequate privacy? Is the marina conveniently located for shopping, banking, etc.? Are marine services available at the marina or nearby? Is the marina convenient to your place of employment? Also consider the location of the specific slip or side-tie you will be renting. Most people prefer being near the end of a walkway dock so that there will be a minimum of walking traffic past their boats. Boat owners who come late at night or early in the morning to run engines for charging batteries are a real nuisance, but it's difficult to find out if there are any of these around until you have already rented a slip. Most people try to avoid slips that are in full view of restaurants and hotels.

Figure 29. *A pushcart facilitates movement of small items around marina docks. (Photo by author.)*

Many people living at side-ties adjacent to boat traffic lanes find
their homes targets for other people's boats. This becomes a special
problem for trimarans, as in many marinas these are the only spaces
available for them. The damage caused by other boats colliding
with moored boats is not always minor. One boat home moored in
Los Angeles Harbor was demolished on a foggy day by a freighter.
Fortunately, no one was aboard the smaller boat at the time.

A number of marina directories for different sections of the United
States are now being published (see Appendix). They include considerable information about each marina, such as the number of slips,
facilities, cost, and whether or not boat living is allowed.

Yacht Clubs

Many yacht clubs have their own marinas, and this is an avenue to
explore when you are looking for a slip. Not all yacht clubs are expensive. While initiation fees are often sizable, your slip fees can be
less than those at neighboring marinas after you are a club member.

Membership in some yacht clubs is open to anyone. At one club
I'm familiar with, slip rental automatically makes you a member.
Other yacht clubs are more exclusive, some of them highly so.
Typically, an applicant has to be recommended by one or more
active members and be voted in as a member. After the initiation
fee, there are generally monthly dues, which vary widely from club
to club, but sometimes they are quite reasonable when the facilities
and benefits are taken into account.

Mooring buoys

Mooring buoys are much more convenient than setting your own
anchor for boat living. Mooring buoys are provided by clubs, boatyards, and municipalities. As a general rule, they are much less expensive to rent than boat slips or side-ties. In some countries it
seems to be the standard arrangement to place buoys so that the
boat can be tied stern to a quay, but this arrangement does not seem
very popular in the United States. In the United States the buoys
usually are placed away from shore and a dinghy is necessary for
shuttling to and from land. Sometimes a single buoy is used and the
boat is allowed to swing a full circle, or the boat may be linked to
both a bow and a stern line.

In some places the boat owner is responsible for obtaining, setting, and maintaining the mooring equipment. A permit may be required. To ensure sound sleep, make certain that the mooring tackle is adequate and properly maintained.

Some people prefer a mooring buoy arrangement to a boat slip in a marina, feeling that it gives more privacy. Some also like the separation from the shore. Rowing a dinghy provides good exercise, and many consider it fun rather than work.

At anchor

Some people live at anchor. This method is especially popular with those on rock-bottom budgets and those who maintain no regular home port. In areas that are not densely populated and have large bodies of protected water, free anchorages abound. In other areas, especially in densely populated spots along the West Coast with few natural harbors, there has been a growing tendency to limit the length of time one may anchor, which in turn eliminates permanent living at anchor. In many places, anchoring is banned altogether.

Important considerations when choosing an anchorage are location, protection from weather and water conditions, type of holding ground, and situation for landing and leaving dinghies. Good anchoring tackle is essential. In some anchorages, anchor lights are not required.

As an example of a free anchorage, the Commercial Basin in San Diego Bay has long been popular with low-budget boat dwellers. There have been many attempts to stop boat living there, on grounds that the anchorage population is made up of undesirable people living in derelict boats, and with the implication that they are responsible for a reportedly high theft rate in the area, use drugs, and harbor wayward minor girls. It is my opinion, however, that these complaints are exaggerated and are another example of bias on the part of some against the boat dweller's way of life. In any case, the laws that reportedly are being violated are unrelated to type of residence. At the time of this writing, the free anchorage is still in existence in San Diego, although there is talk of putting in mooring buoys and prohibiting anchoring. The mooring buoys will rent for "about" $15 a month. I suspect that the price will quickly go up, and soon the free anchorage will be overtaken by the same profit madness as marinas.

Restrictions against living aboard are almost certain to follow, as has already happened in nearby Glorietta Bay, where anchoring is limited to 72 hours in any seven-day period.

Other possibilities

Other locations for boat living do not fit into any neat categories. For example, some people make special arrangements to tie up to a bank, or to a dock, or between a bridge and a piling. I've even come across a few who beach their boats. In well-protected inland waterways, you are likely to see many unique types of moorings for boat homes, and quite likely people are still inventing new ones.

Boating people on the move with no regular home port, who roam as the fancy strikes them, must make do with whatever is available wherever they happen to be.

Dry-land boat storage

In many areas there are provisions for dry-land storage of boats. In some cases this costs as much as or more than renting a marina slip. Some boat dwellers leave their boats in dry storage while they take vacations ashore or go on business trips that will keep them away from their boats for long periods of time.

Figure 30. *The Commercial Basin in San Diego Bay provides free anchorage for many live-aboarders. (Photo by author.)*

10   LIFE IN A BOAT

The term *living aboard* generally means a combination of living in a boat and on land. At a marina slip, access to land is direct; at anchor or offshore mooring buoy, one gets ashore by dinghy; but in either case, most people spend considerable time ashore. It has been said, with considerable truth I believe, that living in a boat makes it possible to take advantage of the best of both water and land living.

Food preparation and storage

The transition from land to boat living almost always causes an increase in appetite, so expect to develop a hearty appetite. However, most people report that they maintain a lower body weight than when living ashore. Apparently their increased activity more than compensates for the added calories.

Some people prepare all or almost all of their meals aboard the boat; others favor eating some or all meals out. Some buy takeout (carry home) food.

In a modern floating home, it is possible to have a kitchen with all of the space and convenience of a typical kitchen ashore.

While food preparation and storage are much the same as in a land house, there may be some problem providing electricity and gas if they are not supplied directly from shore hookups. This may mean having gas bottles filled at intervals (as with "self-contained" trailer houses) and running a generator for a period each day, which requires a supply of fuel, generally gasoline or diesel oil.

In a functional boat, the galley is likely to be considerably more modest. A well-equipped galley might consist of a four-burner stove with oven, a large (by small-boat standards) sink, adequate work and storage space, and a refrigerator with a freezer. Only a few boats have anything more elaborate; many have much less. A minimal galley might have a simple one- or two-burner stove, a tiny sink, extremely limited work and storage space, and little more. Food preparation in a well-equipped galley is not very different from cooking in a house ashore, but it is less convenient and requires greater organization. In a very small galley, hearty meals are still possible, but they take more planning and effort, rather like camp cooking.

The stoves that I've seen used (not necessarily ideal) have ranged from simple one-burner affairs to those with four or more burners and an oven. Fuel, operation, and advantages and disadvantages of the various types are covered in Chapter 4. While the quality of cooking is not always related to the elaborateness of the stove (I've had some delicious meals that were concocted on one-burner stoves), a larger unit can make things easier, so it certainly is recommended.

When shore-supplied electricity is available, many people use small electric appliances, such as hot plates, electric ovens, toasters, and

Figure 31. *Spacious galley on Kayot's Royal Capri houseboat. (Courtesy Kayot Marine Division.)*

percolators. Frequent use is also made of barbecue grills. These can be used on docks, and models with brackets for outward attachment to stern pulpits are also available and used frequently.

Many people get by without refrigerators. Some use iceboxes, either built-in (these come as standard equipment on many stock boats) or portable models. The amount of ice required and how long it will last depend mainly on the size and insulation of the icebox and the surrounding temperature. A 50-pound block of ice can last about a week, give or take a couple of days. Ice is available at or near most marinas, often from vending machines.

But ice is a bother, and some feel it's not worth the trouble. One couple explained it this way: "We're just too lazy to bother with ice. We've learned to get along without it." This means getting by without foods requiring refrigeration, or using up those that do before they spoil.

There's no getting around the fact, however, that a refrigerator can make life easier and more convenient. And I've noticed that people who have lived in boats for a number of years, say five or more, tend to have refrigerators, even those who started out without them. A refrigerator can be added anytime, and many put it off as a someday item until they can afford one. A typical comment from someone who added a refrigerator, "I don't know how I ever got along without one," reminds one of the days when refrigeration was first being used in land houses.

While hot-water systems are becoming more popular, many people still do without them. They wash dishes in cold water or stove-heated water, the latter being the preferred method from the health standpoint.

Pressure water systems are convenient, whether you use the pressure water supply from a dock outlet or a separate pressure pump. A few people use gravity pressure systems. Using the shore water supply directly saves periodic refilling of the boat's water tanks, and also solves the related problem of keeping the water uncontaminated. Boats anchored offshore have to go in to a dock to fill their water tanks. Although it's much less convenient, many people transport water from shore to boat in plastic containers in a dinghy.

If you find hand-operated pumps too inconvenient, one solution is to switch to a foot-operated pump, which leaves the hands free.

In some places sea water can be used safely for dishwashing, but this is seldom the case around marinas and typical anchorages.

When the weather is nice, it's pleasant to have meals, as well as coffee, snacks, and cocktails, outdoors in the cockpit or on the patio deck. Lap trays or trays on stands are handy for use in cockpits, or a cockpit table can be purchased or constructed. Awnings rigged as sun shades turn a cockpit into a patio.

Related to food preparation is garbage and trash disposal. Plastic bags placed inside plastic containers are handy on board. Most marinas and anchorages have a shore collection station nearby. Regardless of the inconvenience, it behooves all live-aboarders (and everyone else) to refrain from disposing of any garbage or trash in the water (yes, you can pollute a great big ocean).

Sleeping

Assuming there are good berths, good ventilation, adequate temperature and humidity control, and calm water, sleeping aboard a boat should not present any special problems. In fact, many people find it better than sleeping ashore.

Sleeping becomes more difficult, of course, if the water is rough. However, most marinas and anchorages are in well-protected waters, so this is rarely a problem. The type of boat slip and the method of mooring are important in marinas with rough-water conditions (see Chapter 9).

Most of the marinas I'm familiar with, including a number of them in large cities, are fairly quiet and peaceful. I recently cruised along the California coast from Santa Barbara to San Diego, stopping over for one or more nights at a number of marinas and anchorages along the way. No extreme noise problems were encountered at any of them, except perhaps at Avalon on Catalina Island. And that was such a pleasant place I didn't really mind. Even Marina del Rey was a refuge from the bustle of Los Angeles, where it is located.

Many people sleep in sleeping bags, at least in the beginning. Two sleeping bags that zip together can be used on a double berth.

It's almost essential that sleeping bags be washable. Those filled with Dacron seem to work well. Sheets made into liners are also a good idea. Disposable sheets are available, but they are too expensive and wasteful for everyday use. However, some people find them convenient for unexpected overnight guests.

While sleeping bags are neat and easy to make up, many boat dwellers prefer sheets and blankets. People who start out with sleeping bags often switch later to standard bedding. It's a good idea to

Figure 32. *Pump-out stations for boat holding tanks are conveniently located at many marinas. (Courtesy Monogram Industries, Inc.)*

sew bottom sheets so that they are form-fitting, especially when the mattresses aren't rectangular. Electric blankets are good for comfortable sleeping in colder climates.

Good ventilation and temperature and humidity, important factors for sleeping comfort, depend on the boat design, how the boat is equipped, and the climate. Short of moving to another area, not much can be done about the climate. However, some people live happily in boats in cold climates, even through long, freezing winters.

Sewage disposal

If your boat has holding tanks, they have to be emptied, of course. Pump-out stations are now available in most marina and anchorage areas. Frequently they are located at fuel docks. Some marinas have their own pump-out stations, but few have hookups at each slip, although these may soon exist in new marinas designed especially for boat dwellings.

Many pump-out stations are charging fees, generally fifty cents or a dollar, for each pump-out. Another possibility, more convenient but also more expensive, is to subscribe to a pump-out service at your slip. A number of concerns are now offering this service.

Figure 33. *When dock boxes are available, they provide extra storage space for boat dwellers' gear. (Photo by author.)*

Storing Possessions Ashore

Most live-aboarders find that their boats (even floating houses) have only a fraction of the storage space their land houses had. Many consider this an advantage, as it encourages, almost forces, one to get rid of excess possessions. Aboard the *Sea Puppy* there has been more than one "get-rid-of-the-junk" campaign.

Some, perhaps most, boat residents make use of shore storage, which exists in many forms. Marinas frequently have a small dock box for each slip. While their capacity is limited, they will hold many maintenance items, such as brushes, sponges, hoses, paints, and varnishes. Each box generally can be padlocked. Fire regulations may prohibit storage of flammable liquids.

A few marinas have other types of storage, such as lockers or rooms inside a building. Additional rent sometimes is charged for these units.

It may be possible to store some items where you work (if you work). For example, I know a couple, both teachers, who live in a

32-foot powerboat and store many of their books at the schools where they teach. As for myself, at various times I have rented small offices, which I have used for my writing and for storage.

In many areas of the United States there are centers that rent various types and sizes of fireproof, secure storage space.

Some people store items at the homes of relatives and friends. Others rent garages. Another possibility is to store some items in a car, van, or camper. For example, a family living near me owns an old bread van. The van no longer runs, so they use it for storage.

There are, then, many solutions to the storage problem for those who stay in one place. For those who like to move about, it's most convenient to limit possessions to what can be carried easily and safely.

Space, privacy, and comfort

Will there be enough room? This question is frequently asked by those contemplating a move from land to boat. The answer depends on a number of things — boat size and arrangement, lifestyles, and the personalities of the people who will be living together.

In Chapters 3 and 4, recommendations were made on the size of the boat home. In practice, many get by with far less than I feel is essential. For example, I know of a few people who have lived for long periods of time in boats with no standing headroom.

Couples who get along well together have found that they have enough room in boats under 30 feet in length. For example, a woman who lives aboard a 28-foot sailboat with her husband said, "At times we do get in each other's way. But we wouldn't trade the feeling of coziness for a mansion of a house where we might live together but never see each other."

And I know a married couple who have been living together aboard a 30-foot sailboat for 15 years, ever since the last of their three children married. They seem as happy together as newlyweds.

Life at close quarters can help a couple get to know each other better, occasionally with disastrous results. For the wrong couple, confined space can serve as a boxing ring. And most of those living together happily in small boats admit that they would like a larger boat (it's called "bigger-boat fever"). However, only a small percentage of this group move back to land for lack of a larger boat.

With children, space becomes more critical. The health and happiness of children are of vital concern, and Chapter 13 is devoted to this subject. Suffice it to say that for the right family in the right boat, it can be a wonderful life, perhaps the best possible. But without adequate space and privacy, it can be catastrophic.

Most boat homes are cozy and comfortable. Some of the most relaxing and comfortable boats I've been on were those with wood-burning cabin heaters. When it's cold outside, there's nothing else quite like it.

Some boat homes have television sets, although many people want to get away from them. Some only use televisions ashore, in marina and yacht club lounges. Television reception is possible in boats, but the quality and quantity vary greatly from area to area.

Visitors and guests

Most boat dwellers enjoy having visitors and guests. Frequently a pot of coffee is kept ready for visitors. In addition to relatives and friends from the "land world," visitors will probably include other live-aboarders. At many marinas and anchorages there is a real community spirit.

Problems with visitors? According to some hosts, there are always those guests who don't know when to leave, especially visitors from the land world: a boat can be such a pleasant place that visitors don't want to go. However, for the most part, if you want visitors, you can have them, yet your privacy will be respected, too. And if visitors ever become a bother, you can always cast off the dock lines and move somewhere else.

Often the size and arrangement of the boat will necessitate shore accommodations for overnight guests. Motels and hotels are commonly located around marinas and anchorages.

Security

Even though entrance to most marinas is by key or key card, this doesn't always prevent things from being stolen from boats. For this reason I feel that theft insurance, preferably a low-deductible policy, is a good idea. Most often only small items are stolen.

Boats should be locked when no one is aboard. Outboard motors should be chained and locked to the boat or, better yet, stored out of sight in a locked compartment. Dinghies are especially vulnerable. When left ashore, they should be chained and locked to a dock or fixed item on shore.

Boat dwellers can and do look out for each other. After you have been at a marina for a while, you will know who belongs and who doesn't. When you are going to be away from your boat overnight or longer, let your neighbors know so that they can keep an eye on your boat.

The same care should be taken as when living ashore to ensure personal safety. Since security at and around different marinas and anchorages varies greatly, it should be taken into consideration when selecting a place to live aboard.

Boatkeeping

Day-to-day boatkeeping is like housekeeping, but much easier. The boat is smaller, and the materials used in her are, in theory, designed for a marine atmosphere, making them more durable. Boatkeeping means washing, scrubbing, sweeping, vacuuming (for safety, only a grounded wet-and-dry vacuum cleaner should be used), mopping, dusting, and so on. It also means keeping everything in its place.

One special problem is mold and mildew. Good ventilation will largely prevent this, but there are still places where mold can start. Especially troublesome are the areas under mattresses that are in use. One way to help prevent this is to prop up the mattresses sideways when they are not being used. If ventilation is poor, mold is likely to be a problem in storage compartments. Methods of providing better ventilation are covered in Chapters 4 and 8.

While routine boatkeeping can be easier than housekeeping, boat maintenance can be much more demanding than upkeep on a land house, especially when the boat is moored in salt water. Boat maintenance, both interior and exterior, is detailed in Chapter 12.

Shore transportation

While most people keep a motor vehicle of one kind or another, many have turned to bicycles and walking for some or all of their transportation. Self-propulsion is more in keeping with the life in a boat.

Figure 34. *The author prepares to stow his collapsible bicycle, a handy item for land transportation. (Photo by author.)*

Many marinas have rules against leaving bicycles on the marina docks and walkways. Some marinas have special areas for bicycle parking, but these sometimes lack security and protection from the weather. At some marinas it is necessary to keep bicycles in your boat. Bicycles are frequently secured on deck. Since they will be subject to severe environmental conditions, it's important to keep the bicycles covered (special plastic covers are available from bicycle shops and discount stores), clean, dry, waxed, and well lubricated. I have found that silicone lubrication works well on bicycles.

Folding bicycles can be stowed below. Many of the manufactured models have small wheels, however, making them more difficult to pedal than bicycles with 26- or 27-inch wheels. To get around this problem, I added a Bicycle Compactor Kit to a standard bicycle. The complete kit retails for about $13.95. It's manufactured by Girard Engineering Company, 114 Main Street, Tekonsha, Michigan 49092, and is available at many recreational vehicle supply stores. Installation is simple. The frame is cut into two sections with a tube cutter or hacksaw, and special couplings are epoxy-bonded in place. The compacted bicycle is easily stowed below, even in my small sailboat. When marina hopping, I take the bicycle along for use as shore transportation.

Buses and other public transportation are another possibility. By walking, bicycling, and taking public transportation, I've managed to live without an automobile, and I'm much happier in the bargain. I just wish more people felt the same way, so that life would no longer center around motor vehicles.

Water transportation

In some areas water transportation can be used. For example, one can go shopping by dinghy. Although it is somewhat unusual, a few places have water-taxi service. And I know of one man who motors in his boat to his place of employment, which happens to be at a boatyard.

Laundry

Most people do their laundry at laundromats, which are located around many marinas and anchorages. Some floating homes have complete laundry facilities, but this is rare in other types of boats. I know of a few people with small boats who use small washing machines designed for recreational vehicles.

The rigging and lifelines on most boats will serve as clotheslines. However, to avoid a bad image, keep your laundry display to a (tasteful) minimum.

Dry cleaners, including coin-operated machines, are often found near marinas and anchorages, but most people keep very few clothes that require dry cleaning. Wash-and-wear clothing is more practical for boat life.

Hanging lockers keep clean clothes unrumpled; a laundry bag or basket can be used for collecting soiled clothes between laundry times.

Mail

For those who stay in one place, mail usually isn't a special problem. Some people use their business addresses, some have post-office boxes, others use the marina as their address. Some marinas have good systems for handling mail, sometimes going so far as to deliver the mail right to the boats; others leave much to be desired. One city-operated marina that I'm familiar with, for example, throws all of the mail in a large box, and that's the end of it as far as they are concerned. If you find your mail, good. If not, that's your problem. A more typical system is to sort the mail into boxes that are located in one area, often inside the marina office.

If you move frequently, getting mail can be a problem. Forwarding addresses left at post offices work well, but only as long as you don't move too many times. General delivery is a possibility, but some who have tried this report unsatisfactory results. Perhaps a better solution is to maintain a permanent mailing address at the home of a friend or relative.

Receiving mail when cruising, especially outside the United States, is a major logistical problem (see Chapter 15).

Shopping and banking

Stores and shopping centers are found near most marinas and anchorages, making shopping a routine matter.

Some people who change locations frequently have found it convenient to maintain bank accounts in one place and then to bank by mail. Many savings and loan associations offer simple systems for making deposits and withdrawals by mail. A bank with many branches makes check-cashing easier.

Pets

Regulations on keeping pets vary greatly from area to area. Many marinas do not allow pets; others say that the pets must be on a leash when not on the owner's boat. In areas where slips are difficult to obtain, regulations against pets are almost certain to be in effect.

Many pet owners seem to think that having a pet is a divine right, and they fail to take other people into consideration. A barking dog, for example, can quickly make his owner unpopular, to say the least, with the neighbors, especially in a crowded marina.

In spite of all the problems involved, some people still feel that pets are worth the trouble. Cats generally are more suitable boat pets than dogs, at least from the point of view of the neighbors.

People cruising with pets may face additional problems when venturing outside the United States, including complicated forms to be filled out, confinement of pets to the boat, and sometimes quarantine.

11 MAKING A LIVING

While the vast majority of boat dwellers in the United States probably make their living much as they would if they were living on land, some have sought out alternative means of support.

Regular job or profession

For the many people who continue in the same job or profession they had while ashore, moving to a boat is much like moving from one house to another. In some cases the marina location is more convenient to the place of employment; in others, less. I know of a number of people who commute long distances in order to be able to live in a boat rather than in a house.

Some people find new jobs nearer to the marina or anchorage where they live. For example, two teachers I know applied for positions in a number of areas where living aboard would be possible. Finally, they both found teaching assignments in the San Diego area, where they now live in a 41-foot sailboat. Of course, the feasibility of doing something like this depends on many factors. In a tight job market, switching jobs may not be possible or practical, but it's certainly something to consider.

Incomes from retirements and other sources

There are a number of people who do not work yet are able to support themselves aboard a boat. Many with money have taken to boat life as a way to enjoy their freedom from work.

In some cases, the money comes from inheritances, in other cases from investments. I've heard of several instances in which a person has sold out a business and used the money to support a "nonworking" life aboard a boat. The basic idea — and it's gaining popularity — is to achieve independence from work or job obligations.

Many people live on retirement incomes. This is often possible on a small income, especially if the boat is paid for. I know of several people who live solely on social-security money. Retirement incomes generally do not restrict one to a limited area, as a job can, so many retired boat people migrate southward in the winter and northward in the summer. Many add to their incomes with part-time work and various craft and freelance endeavors.

Part-time and temporary jobs

Working part-time can mean making enough money to get by, while at the same time having more freedom to enjoy the live-aboard life. Often the only sacrifices are of meaningless or useless or destructive possessions — such as automobiles — which seem to be the goals of too many people. Think, for example, about the reduction in the number of working hours that a switch from an automobile to a bicycle could mean.

Cruising people often depend on temporary jobs, working only long enough to replenish the kitty, then cruising on again. Some people who remain in one area also follow this system. Part-time and temporary jobs are often available around marinas and anchorages.

Jobs related to boating

Many boat dwellers have jobs related to boating. There are employment opportunities in this area for both the semiskilled and the skilled. Typical jobs involve working for boatbuilders and in boatyards, selling for boat brokers or dealers, working in marine supply stores, and working in one of the many other marine services, such as radio and electronics or boat maintenance.

Teaching is another possibility. In many boating areas there are schools that need teachers for skills and activities such as navigation, sailing, skin and scuba diving, and even boatbuilding. Opportunities are available at both public and private schools. I know one man, for example, who supports his wife and himself by teaching navigation classes in an adult-education program.

Some people work in boat-design offices, since many of the top boat-design firms are located in boating areas. Even boat designers who eventually hope to have their own businesses typically begin their careers by working for established designers.

Self-employment

Some people have even started their own businesses. Often, but not always, these are related in some way to boating. One man, for example, started a business in used marine hardware and equipment. He rented what was once a house that was rezoned for business purposes. With a minimum of investment, he bought some used marine equipment to get started. As the business developed, he continued to buy items outright, but much of his merchandise is now sold on a commission basis. For three or four months each year, he and his family cruise to Mexico, while someone takes over his business temporarily.

The possibilities for marine-related businesses are almost endless. For example, I've known people who have successfully launched marine radio and electronics businesses, holding-tank installation firms, boat brokerages, restaurants, and fiberglass repair services. A bottom-cleaning business is also a good one for someone living in a marina. Many of these businesses can be started with a minimum of capital.

I should also mention that I've seen several such businesses fail. One of these was a correspondence course in navigation that a man and his wife tried to start, but they had neither the capital nor the know-how to make it work.

Some businesses, such as sailing and skin- and scuba-diving schools, involve so many legal problems that they are difficult to operate profitably on a limited basis. Insurance costs can be prohibitive, as is often the case if you want to teach sailing with your own boat. For this reason, many prefer to work for established businesses in these areas rather than attempt to start their own.

Various types of freelance occupations, many of which can be undertaken aboard boats or operated from them, are popular means of support. Freelance writing and photography are two. I have supported myself for three and a half years by freelance writing, with perhaps a quarter of my output on the subject of boating and the remainder on a number of other subjects. I also do some photography.

Some of the most famous world-cruising sailors — Eric and Susan Hiscock, among others — have supported their ventures for many years in this manner. However, I would caution anyone starting out not to depend on writing as the main means of support. And if you have been unable to make money from writing before living aboard, it is unrealistic to expect to do so once you have moved to a boat. A boat is not always an ideal writing studio, at least not for me. While I have done perhaps half my writing over the past several years aboard my boat, it has sometimes been inconvenient, especially when I have had to store large amounts of resource materials. For this reason, I've sometimes rented small offices on shore. My boat is small, however, and a larger boat probably would have enough storage. I've read that the Hiscocks even do their photo processing aboard.

Other popular freelance work includes boat maintenance, interior decorating, boatbuilding and repairing, and marine electronics. Sometimes the people had the skills beforehand, but many picked them up afterward. Making a living by freelancing depends not only on the kind and amount of skill, but also on the demand for the particular services. Also, business regulations and unions may not allow certain businesses.

I've heard of a number of people who make their living by chartering. While I've had no first-hand experience with chartering, it seems to have many advantages. But there are many problems involved, too — primarily difficult customers and expensive insurance. Also, you would need a fairly large boat with suitable accommodations to make this undertaking practical. A few people do make enough money chartering during the tourist season to support themselves aboard their boat for the rest of the year.

12 MAINTAINING YOUR BOAT

I know of no boat that is completely maintenance-free. Even fiberglass and ferrocement boats, despite advertising to the contrary, require some maintenance. Some boats, of course, require much more work than others. Wood and metal boats, for example, generally require more maintenance than fiberglass boats of the same type and size. And more serious problems are likely to develop in wood and metal boats from lack of maintenance than in fiberglass or ferrocement boats, where much of the work may be cosmetic. However, looks are important, too. A boat is a big investment, and it pays to keep her in top condition.

The purpose of maintenance is to preserve the boat, or, more specifically:

(1) To maintain appearance
(2) To prevent deterioration
(3) To keep everything in working order
(4) To repair defects and damage

Boats are in a more hostile environment than houses ashore, especially boats in salt water. Some of the villains are corrosion (both chemical and physical), electrolysis, friction, and radiation. Certain materials, of course, are more immune to some or all of these factors than others. Fiberglass, for example, is not generally affected by teredo worms, dry rot, or electrolysis. However, remember that fiberglass boats are often a combination of many materials, and what these materials are and how they are combined will have a large effect on the amount of maintenance required.

As long as I've had my Westerly Warwick, the total annual cost for maintenance, including annual haul-outs, has averaged less than $150 a year. But to keep the costs this low, I have had to do most of the work myself. If I had paid someone to do this work, the cost would have been considerably more, but I have no way of estimating how much more. Except for the bolted-on, cast-iron twin keels, which require considerable upkeep in comparison with fiberglass boats with bonded-in internal ballast, I think my boat could be classified as easy to maintain. I notice that the small amount of wood trim, which is teak, and the outboard motor require a disproportionate amount of the maintenance time.

What's involved in maintenance

Most of the people I have known do their own maintenance work. Only a few pay to have the work done. In boating areas there are often individuals and firms that will do maintenance for you, or you can pay to have some of the more difficult work done and then do the remainder yourself.

In addition to the routine maintenance jobs that can be done when the boat is in the water, most boats require at least one careening or haul-out a year, and sometimes two or three, for bottom-cleaning and painting.

Boating people seem to have many different ideas about how best to tackle the maintenance of their boats. Some, for example, work at it every day, always keeping their boats bright and shiny. Others tend to let things go for a while, then go at it all at once. Either system can be satisfactory. However, with the wait-a-while, all-at-once method, it's important that the job be tackled before real damage occurs. Preventive maintenance is the key to success aboard a boat, since a boat is less forgiving than a house ashore.

Basic jobs

Keeping the exterior of the boat clean is a continual process. The tools are a bucket, sponges, brushes, mops, rags, and a biodegradable boat soap. If water is piped to the mooring, a hose will make things easier. Otherwise, use whatever water the boat is floating in. While cleaning methods vary somewhat with different boat materials, the common procedure for the topside of most boats is: water down; scrub with soapy water and a sponge, brush, mop, or rag; rinse; then dry with rags, although the last step is often omitted.

Special cleaners, polishes, and waxes are often used on fiberglass.

Use abrasive cleaners and polishes carefully, as they may remove some of the gel coat.

The time between bottom-paintings can generally be prolonged somewhat by periodic scrubbing and scraping while the boat is in the water. Some of the bottom surface can be reached from a dock or dinghy with a long-handled scrub brush. For most boats, however, it will be necessary to go under the water to get all of the bottom cleaned. A diving mask used with or without a snorkel or scuba gear is typical equipment for the task. A wet suit is a decided asset in cold waters. Around most marina and anchorage areas, there are always "divers" soliciting bottom work. Arrangements can usually be made for a one-time job or for periodic cleanings.

Permanently moored floating houses with fiberglass or other plastic underwater sections can often go for long periods of time without bottom-cleaning or painting, since a smooth bottom isn't required

Figure 35. *Boat washing is a simple task when there is a dockside water supply. (Photo by author.)*

for boating performance. However, some owners of floating homes regularly clean the underwater surfaces.

Most boats require at least some painting and/or varnishing from time to time, and a system has to be devised for keeping painted and varnished surfaces in good condition. Since paint generally lasts longer than varnish, some people paint over some of the brightwork. (Interior painting requires special planning. One method is to take a vacation ashore during the painting session. Some people, however, manage to live amid the mess and odor.)

Besides the above tasks, there are a number of other jobs: taking care of engines and other mechanical gear; maintaining spars, rigging, sails, and fittings on sailboats; repairing and servicing plumbing, pumps, electrical systems, electronic equipment, and interior furnishings.

Books devoted to maintenance are listed in the Appendix. Also, stock boats and manufactured gear often come with maintenance and repair manuals.

Bottom-cleaning and painting

Boatyards with haul-out equipment are located in most marina and anchorage areas. However, since there is generally a charge involved, some people find other ways of careening for bottom work, perhaps alongside a jetty in tidal waters.

Charges for boatyard haul-outs and methods of hauling vary, but in most cases you pay for the out and in, plus the number of days the boat is in the yard. Floating-dock lifts are generally more expensive than rail systems, but not always.

Boatyards will generally allow you to do your own work, and even live in your boat while working, but check before you have them haul your boat out. Also, you can usually have friends help you, but in many cases a fee must be paid to the yard if you hire professional help not connected with the boatyard. If the boatyard does the bottom-cleaning and painting, you may be charged according to the boat length, or by the hour. The bottom paint usually is extra if it is furnished by the yard.

Many yards now have steam-cleaning equipment. One yard I'm familiar with charges $11.50 per hour to do steam-cleaning. For many boats, an hour of steaming is ample for cleaning the entire bottom, and this can save you half a day or more of scrubbing and scraping by hand.

Before hauling out, have everything organized and ready. Many boatyards have weekend specials with a set price for going out on Friday and back in on Monday. This is plenty of time for most routine bottom-cleaning and painting, provided you have everything ready and know exactly what you are going to do.

Basic steps are: cleaning and scraping, sanding, priming if required, and applying bottom paint. With some bottom paints, the boat will have to be back in the water within a certain number of hours after the paint has been applied, or the paint will lose some of its effect. Follow the manufacturer's instructions.

During most haul-outs there usually are a variety of other jobs that need to be undertaken. For example, through-hull valves should be greased and zincs replaced. This is also the time to check for any underwater damage and make necessary repairs, or make any modifications that would require a haul-out.

Repairs

Minor repairs are but a short step from routine maintenance, and they often are considered a part of regular maintenance. Certain defects are common in stock boats. For example, cracks and crazing in the gel coat frequently appear in stress areas, especially in areas where stiffening is inadequate. Many boat owners can make these repairs themselves. Techniques are detailed in a number of books (see Appendix).

Making repairs on some floating houses and houseboats sometimes involves techniques and materials like those used in the construction of houses or mobile homes, and generally this work is simpler than typical boat work.

Figure 36. *The* Sea Puppy *undergoes a bottom cleaning with a boatyard's steam-cleaning equipment. (Photo by author.)*

13   CHILDREN IN A BOAT

I've heard strong opinions both for and against bringing up children aboard boats. Large, modern floating homes fall outside the range of this argument, as living in these is little different from living in waterfront homes, which generally are considered ideal environments for children.

Of primary concern are the safety, health, happiness, and education of the children. Let's first consider a boat that is more or less permanently moored in one location, except perhaps for occasional boating and vacation cruising. In other words, the boat has a home port.

The size of the boat is important. While I'm sure there are people who will disagree, I feel that a minimum requirement for each child is to have his or her own private room, which in the case of a boat should be a closed-off, separate compartment. In turn, I feel that the parents also need their private room, and that the insulation and sound properties of the boat should be such that there is more than just visual privacy. It almost always takes a boat with at least the interior space of a 30-foot houseboat to meet these requirements.

This is not to say that I haven't seen families, even with a number of children, living in boats in what amounted to one room. I *have* seen it, and it always saddens me. I recall my own childhood and realize the value of privacy, of having my own room, and I can't help but think that this group living will have an adverse effect on the children. But this is only an opinion, and it's up to the parents to decide.

For a family with very young children or a baby, a marina slip has many advantages over an offshore mooring; in fact, I feel that the slip is almost essential. Consider the difficulties of using the dinghy to get back and forth to shore. Before children are allowed to use the dinghy alone, they should be competent at both handling the dinghy and swimming.

Even at a marina slip, babies and very small children require a number of special considerations. Will it be possible to provide the constant supervision necessary for safety? Many parents devise leashes and safety harnesses for mobile babies and small children, but is this really practical? How will it affect the children?

A good, safe play area on shore close to the marina is a good idea: time should be spent away from the confined space of the boat each day. Also, try to find a marina where there are other people with children the same ages as yours, since children need playmates. If your children are the only ones living in a boat in the area, consider how they will be accepted by other children who live on land.

If the children seem unhappy or maladjusted, a move ashore might be advisable. However, since many children seem to enjoy living aboard boats, this is seldom necessary. Sometimes a cause of trouble is a child's fear that boat living is abnormal and will make him or her an outsider. Fortunately, the opposite is often the case. Land children usually think someone who lives aboard a boat is lucky, and most boat children have many friends on shore who enjoy playing around the marina and the boat.

In some cases everything goes well until the children reach a certain age; then problems begin. For example, a teenager may feel suddenly that he or she has been missing something. Being a teenager can be difficult, and it is only natural to blame things on whatever is handy; this often happens to be the fact that they are living in a boat.

In most cases you will be considered a resident of the city or county where your boat is located, and thus you are entitled to send your children to local public schools. In some areas there may be some difficulties in this regard, but I've never heard of any insurmountable problems. The only major objection I've encountered is that people living on land sometimes complain that families in boats don't pay their fair share of school taxes.

Families living at anchor must also consider the dinghy trip to and from shore, or to and from school. This can present complications, but many manage it. Children often think rowing a dinghy is fun.

Young children can be taught a number of safety skills, such as:

(1) How to put on and use a life preserver
(2) How to throw and use a life ring or ring buoy
(3) How to use a fire extinguisher
(4) How to swim, even with clothing

There are many other skills — dinghy-sailing, rowing, fishing, and skin-diving — that can also be taught to young children. (These

recreational activities are covered in more detail in Chapter 14.)
Children must also learn "shipboard" living, such as the operation
of the head, the use of lights, stowage, and good boatkeeping habits.

I do not recommend taking babies and very small children on offshore cruises, certainly not on ocean passages. I realize that babies
have been taken even around Cape Horn in small cruising sailboats,
but I do not see any point to this. Children should at least be old
enough to know what it's all about. Young children probably won't
even remember the voyage, and there are just too many risks involved.
Consider, for example, the potential need for a medical doctor. Or
any one of hundreds of other frightening possibilities. And keep in
mind that a number of world cruises have ended in disaster, especially
those undertaken in experimental or home-built vessels. Also extremely risky are family voyages undertaken by inexperienced seamen.
Unfortunately, it seems to be the inexperienced who often take along
babies and children. Experienced skippers would probably know
better. To make matters worse, adventure stories are often written
about families who take along children, thus luring others to do the
same.

With teenagers, I think the situation is different. I see no reason
why a year of world cruising would be detrimental, provided that
the teenager wants to do it. But this consideration is important,
since some teenagers might look on it not as a great adventure, but
as a boring experience.

Education of children and teenagers must also be considered if
you are going to be cruising. One solution is for the parents to do
the teaching, often with the help of correspondence courses, but
getting children to cooperate can be difficult, and I think it is unwise
to keep children out of a regular school for more than a year or two.

14 RECREATION

In various sections of this book I've mentioned that one possible disadvantage of boat living is that many possessions and pursuits are impractical or impossible in a boat. On the other hand, there are countless activities ashore that need not be given up, and numerous hobbies and sports are particularly appropriate for boat dwellers. Those discussed below are only a sample of the possibilities, and people are constantly coming up with new ways to adapt unusual activities to boats. Many of these activities are not ideally suited to the limited space, unstable platform, and hostile environment of a boat, but for those who are dedicated, inadequate facilities are better than none. Whenever possible, however, land storage should be used for any equipment subject to very rapid deterioration from the marine atmosphere.

Photography

Photography is an ideal hobby for people in boats, as the surroundings provide many opportunities for picturesque subjects. Probably the vast majority of the boating photographers are amateurs, but some are professionals, and some make all or most of their living with a camera. Many people limit themselves to taking pictures, but some boats are even equipped with small darkrooms. No sensible person would take up darkroom work for the first time in a boat, but an experienced photographer would be able to recognize the limitations of a boat darkroom and adapt his techniques accordingly. A boat darkroom, like a wartime field hospital, must be very simple, and it usually is set up in the toilet compartment. Color-film developing, in which temperatures are critical, is not practical in a small boat.

Special care must be taken to protect photographic equipment from moisture and the marine environment. For a start, more than

one camera has gone overboard. I've had two cameras aboard the
Sea Puppy that have rarely been away from the boat in more than
three years, and they are still in good working order. (I should point
out, however, that my gear is not elaborate, and photography nuts
have been known to laugh at my cameras.) Cameras are protected
best if they are stored in plastic bags with packets of silica gel, which
absorbs moisture. The silica gel turns pale pink when it is soaked,
but it can be dried over heat and reused. Other possibilities are watertight cameras and watertight camera cases, such as those used for
underwater photography.

Do not store film in a boat, and especially in a camera, for long
periods of time. Color film is particularly sensitive to salt air.

Arts and crafts

Drawing, painting, model-building, sewing — the possibilities for
creative endeavors aboard a boat seem endless. Some activities require only simple equipment, while others may involve constructing
special tables or workbenches or fitting in extra equipment, such as
a sewing machine. One man, for example, has a drafting machine
connected to the navigating table, where he designs boats. He also
builds models of his designs, doing most of the work at a small work-
bench built in over what was once a quarter berth. Another person
makes and sells nautical items, such as teak-and-rope bookends.

While a boat does not make an ideal artist's studio, many people
make do. Avoid long-term storage of finished art work, and select
painting and drawing materials that can withstand the rigorous abuse.
In some cases, it's the containers that cause the problem, rather than
their contents. Plastic containers are often the solution.

The elements can have a field day on the mechanism of a sewing
machine, so if you bring one aboard, keep it moisture-free, well
lubricated, and covered.

Collections and other hobbies

Some boat dwellers collect things: stamps, rocks, shells, newspaper clippings, postcards, and more. Others take up astronomy,
navigation, marine biology, or other intellectual pursuits that can be
enjoyed in a limited space. Valuable collections should not be taken

aboard boats. Less cherished assemblages of objects that are moisture-sensitive can be stored with silica gel in plastic bags.

I have also seen a couple of unlikely hobbies pursued successfully on boats. One was piano playing, which involved installing a small piano in a fairly large boat. Another was gardening, not on the boat, but on the marina dock alongside the boat — in planter boxes. And one couple I know has permission from their marina's owner to use a small plot of land on shore for a flower garden.

People with a sincere interest in something have a way of fitting it into boat living.

Books, games, and other on-board entertainment

Books tend to deteriorate rather rapidly in boats, and the volumes printed on cheap papers are the most vulnerable. Nonetheless, libraries are an important part of most boat homes. Books about boating, marine life, and navigation share shelf space with other works on a variety of subjects. Be aware of the damage that can result, and plan your library accordingly. I've had some navigation books aboard the *Sea Puppy* for more than three years now, and they are still in usable, if not mint, condition.

Some stock boats come with book or magazine racks, and owners usually add their own if there are none. Keep in mind the fact that books weigh a lot, so you must limit the size of the library if you have a small boat. The concentrated weight of a library all in one area can affect the performance of functional boats, so it may be a good idea to add a number of small bookracks in different parts of the boat rather than a single large one. In functional boats, the racks should have a barrier to keep the books from tumbling out.

Card and board games can be stored easily and are a favorite form of recreation for many boat dwellers, but the games should be inexpensive and kept to a minimum. They are susceptible to moisture, so try to find waterproof plastic versions. If you use paper cards, keep them in plastic bags.

Use considerable discretion in deciding what electronic equipment to include among your possessions. A boat is no place for expensive and sensitive sound and visual electronic instruments. Radios, televisions, and stereo-tape players should be portable and inexpensive, except, perhaps, for radios specially designed for marine use. Tapes can be stored in plastic bags, but large tape collections and long-term storage should be avoided. If you plan to store battery-powered gear for any length of time, be sure to remove the batteries beforehand.

Fishing

It is only natural that fishing should play an important part in many boat dwellers' lives. Most of them fish mainly for fun and recreation; but there are some sea bums who go hungry when the fish stop biting. Fishing methods, equipment, and bait depend on the type of fishing, area, season, and regulations. A fishing license is often required. You can fish from your boat at its mooring, or "go fishing" where the fancy takes you.

Figure 37. *Many marinas feature dinghy racks. (Photo by author.)*

Swimming, diving, surfing

Being a good swimmer is important for safety. Once you can swim, fins, snorkel, and diving mask are all you need for skin diving. Wet suits can make diving fun in colder waters: in many places it's a year-round sport. For those who want to try scuba diving, professional instruction and certification are recommended.

Many people extend their diving activities to spearing fish, looking for sunken treasures, and underwater photography.

Surfing is popular in some areas. For example, many boats along the West Coast of the United States have surfboards secured on deck or stowed below, which they use frequently. Most wear wet suits.

Dinghies and other small craft

In addition to getting you to and from shore, dinghies can provide considerable recreation. Many people, especially children, seem never to tire of them. Sailing dinghies, which often can be used for rowing, too, add to the fun, and the higher cost of the sailing dinghy may well prove to be a good investment. Some rowing dinghies can be converted to sailing models with a sailing kit purchased from the manufacturer. Many marinas provide dinghy racks, where you may store your dinghy. Some live-aboarders keep other special-purpose boats, perhaps a runabout for water-skiing or a class-racing sailboat.

15 CRUISING

Some people keep their boats moored to the same dock year after year, perhaps moving them only for a haul-out and bottom-painting from time to time. Some boat homes are so firmly connected and dependent on shore connections at a marina slip that cruising is impractical. For instance, the refrigerator may be inoperable without the shore power connection. But the vast majority of people living in functional boats spend at least some time away from the mooring. This may mean going out fishing, making a short day-cruise, overnighting, taking a vacation cruise, or world-cruising. A few make world-cruising a way of life. Some, like Eric and Susan Hiscock, are well known through their writings, but many others follow this way of life without publicity. Members of The Seven Seas Cruising Association must live aboard their boats to remain members, and many have been cruising about the world for years.

The cost

Cruising on a limited basis can be as inexpensive as living in a home port; the cost depends mainly on your style of cruising and the area and boat you're in. Anchoring out free can greatly reduce the cost. Daily guest marina slips cost considerably more than permanent monthly rentals. The cost of operating the boat, of course, also must be counted. Under sail, it can be quite minimal; with a large powerboat, considerable. Power at slow speeds is generally much less expensive than at high speeds. With care, those who cruise continuously in the United States can keep the cost down, even when they have a relatively high living standard, since the boat is their home anyway, and only the costs of operating the boat and paying marina fees are added to the regular stay-in-one-spot budget.

And at the economical extreme, in California there are the hundreds of sea bums (or boat bums, as they are called), who own little more than an old boat, almost always a sailboat, often without an engine, and live on a minimum budget, generally working as little as possible. It is my impression that they fare much better than their land counterparts, enjoying their freedom at very little cost. It is interesting to note that many professional people have taken up this life; many of the others are there by choice, too, not because they can't do anything else.

The cost of world-cruising has risen alarmingly in recent years, especially when the cost of a suitable boat is taken into account. A world-cruising 32-foot sailboat, for example, will probably cost twice as much today as it would have only a few years ago. To complicate the matter, very few boats, in spite of advertising claims, are suitable for world-cruising. Of course, exactly what boat is best is a highly debatable issue, and even people with many offshore miles behind them cannot agree. One person, for example, favors a heavy-displacement, long-keel double-ender. Someone else is in favor of a light-displacement boat with a fin keel and spade rudder. Still another successful cruiser believes in the trimaran. And so on. Many of these sailors have written books on world-cruising. One captivating book on the subject is Joshua Slocum's *Sailing Alone Around the World.*

Cruising outside the United States is not carefree. In many countries the novelty of small boats coming from faraway places has long since worn off, and the welcome mat is no longer as visible as it once was. Many countries are now charging cruising people heavy fees. Insurance rates rise sharply when you leave the United States, and many insurance companies are not even interested. In general, after you leave the United States, you must be more independent and self-contained.

While there may be many obstacles between the dream and reality of boat living, they are nothing compared to those involved in turning the dream of sailing around the world in a small boat into a reality. Many still dream the dream, however. One couple spent years on it, saving the money, reading and studying, then buying a boat and equipping her. Finally there came the day of departure, without a day offshore in their experience. They had done their practicing in the shelter of a protected bay. A week later they were back, the boat was for sale, and two people wanted to get as far from the sea as possible. Another shattered dream, but they came closer to the real thing than most people do.

Against all odds, each year it seems that more and more people succeed — in spite of the higher costs and cooler welcome to be found in many parts of the world. World-cruising is still an intriguing proposition, and I must admit that I hope to do it myself someday.

Overnighting and vacation cruising

Most boating people content themselves with something less than world-cruising, mainly overnighting (spending one night away from the usual mooring) and vacation cruising.

For any cruise, make certain that your boat is suitable both in design and construction and has the necessary equipment for the waters where you will be cruising. For some boats moored in certain areas, this can mean very limited cruising. For example, a houseboat

Figure 38. *Marina and anchorage in Mazatlan, Mexico — a popular stopover spot for cruising live-aboarders. (Photo by author.)*

might be limited to a small harbor area if it would be unsafe on the open sea.

A first cruise might be merely a night spent at anchor within sight of your marina slip. In any case, make sure that it's well within the range of your boating experience and skill. Then gradually work up to more ambitious undertakings.

Most people enjoy cruising when they are involved, so make sure everyone aboard has a part in the activities. And remember that different people may enjoy different aspects of a cruise. One person may enjoy piloting or sailing the boat, another swimming and relaxing at anchor. Children may prefer the dinghy to the larger boat and exploring an island to moving through the water under power or sail.

Many people spend their vacations cruising. In southern California, for example, a favorite cruise is to go marina-hopping along the coast, staying in guest slips (for a fee) at marinas along the way, or one can cruise to Catalina Island and rent a mooring buoy or anchor. In most other areas there are also popular cruises.

While most marinas charge a daily rate for their slips, it may be possible for members of a yacht club to obtain a free guest mooring at another yacht club. In some areas mooring buoys are available, either free or to rent, and in most areas you can find a place to anchor free.

16 A BOATING EDUCATION

Most live-aboarders want to know more about boats and boating, regardless of their present knowledge and skill. It has often been said that experience is the best teacher, and while there may be considerable truth to this, I feel that actual experience can be supplemented by reading, attending classes, and learning from others.

Experience

Most novices learn a great deal from practice. Of course, there are those who seem unable to learn from experience; they get worse instead of better. Fortunately, they are the exception rather than the rule. Experience may be the result of trial and error, but where safety is concerned, error must be kept to a minimum.

In any case, it often takes some experience before other methods of learning become meaningful. For example, a how-to book on sailing may have little meaning until the reader has experienced some actual sailing.

Many aspects of living aboard and using a boat require skill in addition to knowledge. Planing the edge of a board, for example, requires not only knowing how to do the job (knowledge), but also skill in handling the plane. Docking a boat also demands both skill and knowledge if it is to be done competently.

Skill is gained through practicing a task until it becomes habit. Skill also requires that the task be performed competently or in an ideal manner. The performance of a task over and over again with poor technique can result in a bad habit. Bad habits are difficult to correct, so much time and effort can be saved by learning it right the first time. For this reason, I believe that there are many instances when it's best not to try to learn completely on your own.

Published material

There is a large body of published material relating to boating, a considerable portion of which is helpful to people living in boats. The Appendix lists magazines, newspapers, books, and other publications for further reference.

Classes

Classes are offered in many subjects useful to boating people.

Coast Guard Auxiliary. Courses in safe boating are taught by qualified Auxiliary members. Announcements about Coast Guard Auxiliary courses are posted in boating areas, and information is given in newspapers and on radio and television. Information can also be obtained by contacting the Coast Guard Auxiliary for your area, or writing the United States Coast Guard Auxiliary, U.S.C.G. Headquarters, 400 7th St., S.W., Washington, D.C. 20591.

Power Squadron. The United States Power Squadron, a nationwide association of boaters, conduct an extensive program of boating instruction as one of their activities. Local squadrons throughout the United States present a basic course consisting of twelve lessons, known as the United States Power Squadron (USPS) Piloting Course. This is open to all boating enthusiasts. More advanced courses are available to members of the Power Squadron. Obtain information about classes in your area by contacting the local Power Squadron, or write to USPS Headquarters, 50 Craig Road, Montvale, New Jersey 07645. Boating stores in your area should also be able to supply information about courses.

Red Cross and YMCA. The American Red Cross and the YMCA frequently offer courses in boating safety, as well as other useful courses, such as swimming, water safety, and first aid.

Public and private schools. Many community colleges and adult-education programs offer courses for no fee or a very nominal one. Offerings often include navigation, various shop courses with skills applicable to boatbuilding and maintenance, and electronics, as well as a variety of other courses, such as photography, art, and writing.

A number of commercial schools offer courses in a variety of boating subjects, such as navigation, seamanship, sailing, powerboat operation, cruising techniques, and marine electronics. Most of these schools charge a healthy fee, so check the offerings of the public schools first, as a large tuition fee is no guarantee that the instruction will be better or even as good. For example, in one area I'm familiar with, the celestial navigation courses offered free by the adult-education program are generally considered to be superior to those offered by a commercial firm, which charges a $100 enrollment fee.

However, many commercial schools do offer quality instruction, and courses such as offshore sailing may not be available elsewhere. Check the reputation of the school before paying your money. These schools are usually listed in phone books.

Correspondence courses

Courses in a number of subjects related to boating — such as basic boating, seamanship, navigation, marine electronics, yacht designing, and piloting — are offered by correspondence. It should be pointed out that many people are unable to benefit from this type of study. Some sources indicate that fewer than 25 percent of those who enroll in technical (nonboating) correspondence courses finish them. I'm not sure what the completion rate is in boating courses, but I have a feeling that it must also be low.

For many reasons, correspondence study is difficult to sustain. The advertised advantage that you can study at your own convenience is often the downfall of the idea. Many people find it more convenient not to study at all. The lessons themselves seldom seem as exciting as the brochures lead you to expect.

Yet, there are a few people who have profited greatly by correspondence study, and some have even used this method to develop skills for earning a living. For example, I know a yacht designer who learned by taking a correspondence course. It took him more than two years to complete the course. He is the type of person who obviously has a lot of drive, and this was coupled with the facts that he disliked his former job and was extremely interested in designing boats. And he already had a degree in mechanical engineering.

In any case, I recommend that you consider carefully both the course and your ability to profit from this type of study before sending in your enrollment fee or starting on the payment plan. Also, make sure the course is approved by the National Home Study Council, that you fully understand the contract, and that you know what the refund will be should you decide not to finish the course.

Also note that many correspondence schools spend a large part of their budgets on advertising. Some will actually send a salesman knocking on your door. Others will flood you for years with so much material about their courses that one is tempted to enroll just to stop the mailing.

Boating clubs and organizations

A great deal can be learned about boat living from others, by observing and asking questions. Most people are glad to share information and insights. A good place to meet boat dwellers is in boating clubs and organizations, which, in addition to social benefits, can offer access to much information about boating.

In some areas, such as at Marina del Rey in Los Angeles, there are special live-aboarder clubs. If there is none in your area, you may want to start one. The first step is to assemble a group. From there on, everything will probably fall into place.

One national association is the Homaflote Association, P. O. Box 336, Wickford, Rhode Island 02852. Members are required to be boat residents for at least six months of each year. Annual dues, which include a subscription to the newsletter, are $3 at the present time. In August 1975, there were more than 300 members, and the association was growing rapidly.

A number of other national organizations are listed in the Appendix.

APPENDIX

A selected and annotated list of references and information sources that apply to various aspects of boats and living aboard them.

Periodicals

American Boating, 3717 Mt. Diablo Boulevard, Lafayette, California 94549. Applies mainly to western states.

Boating, P. O. Box 2773, Boulder, Colorado 80302.

Family Houseboating, P. O. Box 500, Calabasas, California 91302. Devoted exclusively to houseboating, with much information about living aboard, including interesting personal-experience articles.

Go Boating, 261 W. 6th Street, Miami, Florida 33130. Articles of interest to Florida boat owners.

Lakeland Boating, 412 Longshore Drive, Ann Arbor, Michigan 48107. Articles of interest to fresh-water boaters (power and sail).

Motor Boating & Sailing, P. O. Box 1563, New York, New York 10019.

Multihulls, 91 Newbury Avenue, North Quincy, Massachusetts 02171. Articles on buying, building, living aboard, and cruising.

National Fisherman, 21 Elm Street, Camden, Maine 04843. Covers many aspects of boats and boating. Has large annotated supplement on boating books.

Pacific Skipper, P. O. Box 1698, Newport Beach, California 92663. Has many good articles on living aboard and cruising.

Powerboat, P. O. Box 3842, Van Nuys, California 91407. Has some material that may be of interest to powerboat live-aboarders.

Rudder, 1515 Broadway, New York, New York 10024.

Sail, Institute for Advancement of Sailing, Inc., 38 Commercial Wharf, Boston, Massachusetts 02110.

Sailing, 125 East Main, Port Washington, Wisconsin 53074.

Sea, 551 Channel Street, Marion, Ohio 43302.

Soundings, P. O. Box 210, Wethersfield, Connecticut 06109. Published monthly. Has large section of classified advertising.

Telltale Compass, 18418 South Old River Drive, Lake Oswego, Oregon 97034. Reports on boats and marine equipment. Brands are named.

The Windbag, Westsail Corporation, 1638 Placentia Avenue, Costa Mesa, California 92627. Information about cruising, equipping, and living aboard Westsail boats.

The Woodenboat, P. O. Box 268, Brooksville, Maine 04617. Good coverage of design, construction, maintenance, and repair of wooden boats.

Yachting, Yachting Publishing Corporation, 50 West 44th Street, New York, New York 10036.

Mail-Order Catalogs

These firms will supply customers directly by mail or freight. Most of these charge for their catalogs. Other mail-order firms are listed in buyer's guides and equipment directories.

United States
Al-Sail, Inc., 14 North Street, Hingham, Massachusetts 02043.
James Bliss & Co., Inc., Route 128, Dedham, Massachusetts 02026.
The Boat Locker, Inc., 1375 E. State Street, Westport, Connecticut 06880.
Defender Industries, Inc., 255 Main Street, New Rochelle, New York 10801.
Discount Marine, Inc., P. O. Box 2445, Fort Lauderdale, Florida 33303.
Goldberg Marine, 202 Market Street, Philadelphia, Pennsylvania 19106.
Mail Order Marine, 525 Superior Avenue, Newport Beach, California 92660.
Manhattan Marine & Electric Co., Inc., 116 Chambers Street, New York, New York 10007.
West Products, 161 Prescott Street, East Boston, Massachusetts 02128.

England
Thomas Foulkes, Lansdowne Road, Leytonstone, London, E11, England.
Derry Long and Company, Ltd., 65 East Street, Chichester, Sussex, England.
Captain O. M. Watts, Ltd., 49 Albemarle Street, Piccadilly, London W1, England.

Buying Guides

Boat Owners Buyers Guide, Yachting, 50 West 44th Street, New York, New York 10036. Published annually. An extensive and easy-to-use guide to boats, equipment, and marine services, including where to charter and rent boats, mail-order firms, and schools and instruction in boating.
The Mariner's Catalog, International Marine Publishing Company, Camden, Maine 04843. Published annually since 1973. Essentially a Whole Earth Catalog for boating people. Includes information on rare and unusual items, along with reports on the latest in boats, equipment, tools, books, etc.
Power Boat Annual, 130 Shepard Street, Lawrence, Massachusetts 01843. Information on how and where to buy boats and marine products.
Sailboat & Sailboat Equipment Directory, Institute for Advancement of Sailing, Inc., 38 Commercial Wharf, Boston, Massachusetts 02110. Published annually. A comprehensive guide to sailboats and gear and equipment.

Directories of Marinas, Anchorages, and Boat Rentals

Family Houseboating's Houseboat Rental Guide, Family Houseboating, 10148 Riverside Drive, North Hollywood, California 91602. Covers houseboat rentals in all parts of the United States.
Sea Boating Almanac, 1499 Monrovia Avenue, Newport Beach, California 92663. Three separate editions: The Southern California (from Morro Bay south), Arizona, and Baja Edition; The Northern California (from Morro Bay to the Oregon border) and Nevada Edition; and The Pacific Northwest Edition, which covers Oregon, Washington, British Columbia, and southeastern Alaska. Information about public and private marinas in both coastal and inland waters.

Sunset Where to Go Boating in California, Lane Magazine & Book Company, Menlo Park, California 94025. Information about marinas and boat-rental agencies. Includes the San Francisco Bay and Delta areas.

Waterway Guide, P. O. Box 1486, Annapolis, Maryland 21404. Published annually in three separate editions: Northern Edition covers Atlantic Coastal waters from New York Harbor to Maine/Canada border, up the Hudson River, through the Erie Canal system into Lake Ontario and Lake Erie; Lake Champlain and Richelieu Canal system to Sorel, Quebec; 1000 Islands, St. Lawrence River and Seaway; Rideau Canal to Ottawa; Trent-Severn Waterway to Georgian Bay, with special sections on Long Island Sound, Narragansett Bay, Cape Cod and Islands. Mid-Atlantic Edition covers from New York Harbor south along the Atlantic Coast and via the Intracoastal Waterway and adjacent waters to the Georgia/Florida border, with special sections on Delaware Bay and River, Chesapeake Bay, Sounds and Outer Banks. Southern Edition covers from northern Florida border via Intracoastal Waterway and adjacent waters to the Florida Keys and up Florida's west coast; around the coast of Gulf of Mexico via Intracoastal Waterway to U.S. terminus at Brownsville, Texas, with special sections on St. Johns River, Okeechobee Waterway, and Bahamas information. Each edition lists marinas, fuel stops, and repair facilities. Valuable guide for locating a marina.

Books

A selected and annotated list of books is included here. However, since there are hundreds of other books that will probably also be of interest, this list is intended only as a starting point. A free catalog of over 500 books on boating and marine subjects is available on request from International Marine Publishing Company, 21 Elm Street, Camden, Maine 04843.

Andrews, Howard L., and Alexander L. Russell. *Basic Boating: Piloting and Seamanship.* Englewood Cliffs, New Jersey: Prentice-Hall, Inc., 1964. Good treatment of fundamentals.

Baader, Juan. *The Sailing Yacht.* New York: W. W. Norton & Company, Inc., 1965. Good introduction to all types of sailing craft.

Benford, Jay R., and Herman Husen. *Practical Ferro-Cement Boatbuilding.* Camden, Maine: International Marine Publishing Company, 3rd ed., 1971. Details the construction of a 60-foot ferrocement ketch.

Bingham, Bruce. *Ferro-Cement: Design, Techniques and Application.* Cambridge, Maryland: Cornell Maritime Press, Inc., 1974. A comprehensive source of information for anyone considering ferrocement boat construction. Gives realistic estimates of building time and costs. Has chapter on FER-A-LITE brand synthetic mortar.

Brewer, Edward S., and Jim Betts. *Understanding Boat Design.* Camden, Maine: International Marine Publishing Company, 1971. A valuable starting point for anyone considering buying or building a boat.

BUC New Boat Directory (12th ed., 1974). BUC International Corporation, International Bldg., 2455 E. Sunrise Boulevard, Fort Lauderdale, Florida 33304. Also *BUC's 1974 Used Boat Directory*, Vol. 2, 25th ed., 1974. Price books for boats.

Cairncross, Chris. *Ferro-Cement Boat Construction.* Camden, Maine: International Marine Publishing Company, 1972. Describes the planning, equipment, and techniques necessary for constructing ferrocement boats.

Chapelle, Howard I. *Boatbuilding.* New York: W. W. Norton & Company, Inc., 1941. Extremely valuable for anyone considering buying or building a wood boat.

Cotter, Edward F. *Multihull Sailboats.* New York: Crown Publishers, 1971. Good introduction to catamarans and trimarans.

Duffett, John. *Modern Marine Maintenance.* New York: Motor Boating & Sailing Books, 1973. Complete guide to the maintenance and repair of boats. Stresses modern methods and materials.

DuPlessis, Hugo. *Fibreglass Boats: Fitting Out, Maintenance and Repair.* Tuckahoe, New York: John De Graff, Inc., rev. ed., 1973. Shows how boats are and should be constructed. Valuable for both buyers and builders.

Ferro Corporation. *How to Repair Fiber Glass Boats*, 1969. Ferro Corporation, One Erieview Plaza, Cleveland, Ohio 44114. An easy-to-follow manual with clear illustrations on making repairs.

Gibbs and Cox, Inc. *Marine Design Manual for Fiberglass Reinforced Plastics.* New York: McGraw-Hill Book Company, 1960. Good technical manual.

Harris, Robert B. *Racing and Cruising Trimarans.* New York: Charles Scribner's Sons, 1970. Good introduction to all types of trimarans.

Hiscock, Eric C. *Cruising Under Sail.* New York: Oxford University Press, 2nd ed., 1965. A classic on cruising.

_____. *Voyaging Under Sail.* New York: Oxford University Press, 2nd ed., 1970. This book takes the reader further offshore.

Klingel, Gilbert. *Boatbuilding with Steel.* Camden, Maine: International Marine Publishing Company, 1973. A good book for buyers and builders of steel boats. Includes chapter, "Boatbuilding with Aluminum," by Thomas Colvin.

Lane, Carl D. *The Cruiser's Manual.* New York: Funk & Wagnalls, 1970. A complete handbook of yacht cruising under sail and power.

Malo, John W. *The Complete Guide to Houseboating.* New York: Macmillan Publishing Company, Inc., 1974. Good introduction to all aspects of houseboats and houseboating.

Miller, Conrad. *Your Boat's Electrical System.* New York: Motor Boating & Sailing Books, 1973. Excellent guide to all aspects of electrical systems on boats.

Newcomb, Duane. *The Wonderful World of Houseboating.* Englewood Cliffs, New Jersey: Prentice-Hall, Inc., 1974. Covers both houseboats and houseboating.

Nicolson, Ian. *Small Steel Craft.* London: Adlard Coles, 1971. An excellent introduction to the design, construction, and maintenance of steel boats.

_____. *Surveying Small Craft.* Camden, Maine: International Marine Publishing Company, 1974. A valuable guide for those searching for a live-aboard boat.

Norris, Martin J. *Your Boat and the Law.* Rochester, New York: The Lawyers Co-operative Publishing Company, 1965. Covers boating registration, laws, regulations, and insurance. Includes chapter on the legal aspects of chartering.

Parker, David M. *Ocean Voyaging.* Tuckahoe, New York: John De Graff, Inc., 1974. Good book for those planning offshore and world cruising.

Phillips, Norman. *All About Houseboats.* New York: Motor Boating & Sailing Books, 1972. Guide to houseboats and cruising.

Robinson, William. *The Right Boat for You.* New York: Holt, Rinehart and Winston, 1974. Guide to selecting and buying new and used boats. Covers both sail and power, and has good general introduction to construction materials and hull types.

Toghill, Jeff. *The Boat Owner's Maintenance Manual.* Tuckahoe, New York: John De Graff, Inc., 1971. Covers all aspects of boat maintenance.

Scott, Robert J. *Fiberglass Boat Design and Construction.* Tuckahoe, New

York: John De Graff, Inc., 1973. Introduction to all aspects of fiberglass boat design and construction.

Steward, Robert M. *Boatbuilding Manual*. Camden, Maine: International Marine Publishing Company, 1970. A comprehensive book on building wooden boats.

Street, Donald. *The Ocean Sailing Yacht*. New York: W. W. Norton & Company, Inc., 1973. A compendium of facts on construction, rigging, and outfitting of ocean sailing yachts.

Verney, Michael. *Complete Amateur Boat Building*. New York: The Macmillan Company, 2nd ed., 1967. Covers wood, fiberglass, and metal.

West, Jack. *Modern Powerboats*. Camden, Maine: International Marine Publishing Company, 2nd ed., 1975. Covers powerboat design, construction, and equipment.

Wiley, Jack. *Fiberglass Kit Boats*. Camden, Maine: International Marine Publishing Company, 1973. Covers finishing out bare hulls, with or without component kits. Includes directory of manufacturers of kit boats.

_____. *Modifying Fiberglass Boats*. Camden, Maine: International Marine Publishing Company, 1975. Guide to modifying fiberglass boats.

Willis, Melvin D. C. *Boatbuilding and Repairing with Fiberglass*. Camden, Maine: International Marine Publishing Company, 1972. A how-to book for building and repairing fiberglass boats.

Wynn, Peter. *Foam Sandwich Boatbuilding*. Camden, Maine: International Marine Publishing Company, 1972. A how-to book for building fiberglass boats by the foam sandwich technique.

Zadig, Ernest A. *The Complete Book of Boating*. Englewood Cliffs, New Jersey: Prentice-Hall, Inc., 1972. Covers all aspects of both boats and boating. Includes both power and sailing boats. Contains considerable information of use to live-aboarders.

Organizations, Clubs, and Associations

American Boat and Yacht Council, Inc., 15 E. 26th Street, New York, New York 10010. Membership is composed of individuals, corporations, and groups devoted to development of safety standards for boats and equipment. Publishes a book, *Safety Standards for Small Craft.*

American Boating Association, 3067 Douglas Road, Miami, Florida 33133. For boat owners. Marine insurance is included in membership.

American National Red Cross, 17th and D Streets, N.W., Washington, D.C. 20006. Provides classes in swimming, water safety, first aid, and small-craft operation. Publishes instructional booklets.

Boat Owners Association of the United States, 8111 Gatehouse Road, Falls Church, Virginia 22042. A number of services, including group-rate insurance, boat financing, book and magazine discounts, and correspondence courses on seamanship and piloting, are available to members. Has monthly publication, *Boat/U. S. Reports.*

Boat Owners Council of America, 401 N. Michigan Avenue, Chicago, Illinois 60611. Publishes magazine on boating safety, facilities, and legislative reporting for members.

Cruising Club of America, c/o Chubb & Sons, 90 John Street, New York, New York 10038. For those interested in cruising.

Homaflote Association, P. O. Box 336, Wickford, Rhode Island 02852. An informal national association for live-aboarders. Publishes a newsletter.

Houseboat Association of America, P. O. Box 7285, Asheville, North Carolina 28807. A national organization. Offers many services to members. Publishes a bimonthly newsletter.

International Ferro-Cement Society, 235 West Street, Annapolis, Maryland 21401. A clearing house for information on ferrocement boatbuilding.

National Boating Federation, Bryn Athyn, Pennsylvania 19009. Information exchange for amateur boaters. Has quarterly publication, *The Lookout*.

Seven Seas Cruising Association, P. O. Box 6354, San Diego, California 92106. Publishes a bulletin of letters written by members.

United States Coast Guard, Headquarters, 400 7th Street, S.W., Washington, D.C. 20591.

United States Coast Guard Auxiliary, U.S.C.G. Headquarters, 400 7th Street, S.W., Washington, D.C. 20591.

United States Power Squadrons, P. O. Box 345, Montvale, New Jersey 07645. Private organization dedicated to boating enjoyment and education. Offers courses to members and general public.

The Wooden Boat Club, 92 Hickory Grove Drive, Larchmont, New York 10538. Offers discount buying privileges to members. Publishes a quarterly magazine.

INDEX